BURIED TREASURES

A MOTHER'S LOVE LETTERS
TO HER CHILDREN

SHANNON LOUCKS

Printed in the United States of America.

ISBN: 979-8-9868998-1-7 (paperback)
ISBN: 979-8-9868998-0-0 (ebook)

Edited by Speak Write Play LLC
Cover art by Cassidy Baillie
Interior design by FormattedBooks

Dedicated to all the women in my life who have shown me how to mother from a place of love and deep reflection. Thank you for holding me, inspiring me but most of all for knowing I could do it.

CONTENTS

THE EARLY YEARS

MIDDLE YEARS

TEENS AND YOUNG ADULTS

TO YOU, DEAR READER

Hello Dear Reader,

Parenting isn't Hallmark's version of love. It's actually unconditional love with all its thorns and delicious roses. Shortly after my first child was born, I sat weeping in the bathtub. It was the guttural sort of weeping one does in the throes of grief. I was not expecting it at all. I had watched enough *A Baby Story* on TLC to know that motherhood was supposed to be a wonderful blessing filled with joy at welcoming a child into the world. Don't get me wrong, I was profoundly joyful at meeting my son, but I could not ignore the ache that came alongside it. At that moment, I believe I began to understand that parenting is built on the foundation of great love, which always includes joy and sorrow. It is like the moment a child takes their first steps and the onlookers' eyes fill with tears—tears of celebration for the now toddling child, with a hint of nostalgia for the baby they will never be again.

It was no longer just about me; it was also about the tiny human I had welcomed into the world. This book began with reflections on what it took along the way to undo parts of myself to be present for my children.

Before we begin, let me thank you for loving that child of yours in a way that puts the space between you as the highest priority. I know it is not easy to walk in a world that both undervalues children and the parents who are raising them. I see you over there unpacking your preconceived ideas of parenting as you read this. I see you showing up in your best version of yourself to tend to your precious children. I am there with you in the messy place of growth and change that calls us to transform over and over again with each new phase our children enter. You are not alone, and you have what it takes to trust the unique connection that exists between you and your child. Lean into the love and watch it grow you both into the humans the world needs.

This unique connection we have with our children is what makes us push through each challenge and commit again to the unconditional love between us. It is within the letters to my children in this book that I give you a sneak peek into that very connection and how it served me on my mothering journey.

This book does not need to be read cover to cover. In fact, I invite you to find the letters that call to you and flip right to them. Your life is full enough already, so just take them in one letter at a time as you need to fill your own love bucket.

WHY I'M WRITING TO YOU, MY CHILDREN

Hello My Loves,

Every time I sit down in front of the screen to gather my thoughts to tell you of what it is to be your mother, I find myself at a loss for words. This will likely make you both laugh considering I am the wordiest amongst us all. I thought instead I would write you a series of love letters, and perhaps when you look at them through the lens that is my eyes, you might come to understand how it is I became your mother.

There are so many lessons you have taught me throughout our journey together—through the demons you had me face, the love that rushed to the surface, the examples you set, or the literal words you spoke to me while we lived side by side.

Throughout my own life, writing has been a deep source of healing—a way I could connect with a part of my brain that was generally inaccessible through the noise of daily demands. I wrote my first poem at nine years of age. It was to my grandad who had died; I was missing him terribly. When I look back now, I realize it was a love letter.

And when Gramps (my dad) started to work in another city, I wrote him notes for each day that he was away. I would tuck them in his suitcase for him to discover. Upon his death, I found each one of those notes hidden inside a green box with my twelve-year-old handwriting on it. Once again, I discovered these were love letters to him from a daughter finding her way through young adolescence.

Since then, even my Uncle Gerry has returned letters to me that I wrote to him while I was growing up. At her wedding, Cousin Marie read from one of the letters I had sent her as a young girl. So, I suppose I have been writing love letters my entire life. The letters, I now know, were as much for me as they were for the people I sent them to.

I have been far from a perfect mother. What I am, and continue to be, is a mother committed to letting our relationship be more important than the stress balls that threaten to come between us.

You two have been ridiculously gracious in the ways you have let me tell our stories to others who might stand a chance of learning something about their own way of raising humans. I hope these letters might help you to understand why that felt so deeply important to me.

Yours in love,
Mama

THE EARLY YEARS

Hello again, Dear Reader,

Let's get started with the early years of parenting. Shortly after I gave birth to my first child, I went to the grocery store.

The cashier said to me, "Oh, you had the baby. You must be so happy that he is here."

I nodded and smiled, then gave a socially acceptable response. While internally I thought, he was a lot easier to take care of on the inside.

From feeding to sleeping and everything in between, we are called to pull up new skills while feeling exhausted and vulnerable. Nowhere else in our world are we asked to do a critically important job without any on-the-job training or how-to manuals.

Join me in the following pages as we delve into these big topics and how liberally applying unconditional love kept me focused on the connection I was building with my children.

PREGNANT IN PARIS

Hello My Loves,

I feel like I met you the moment I knew you were growing inside of me. With you, my firstborn, it started with a trip to Paris.

Dad and I landed at Charles de Galle Airport late on the evening of September 10, 2001. Walking through the gates, past empty luggage belts, and out into the street, we were certain we had somehow entered the country illegally. We had never experienced such an easy immigration process. It is true that it was before 9/11 and that we were both limited in our experience of entering other countries.

We swung our matching blue Mountain Equipment backpacks, freshly stitched with Canadian flags, onto our backs before hitting the dark streets in search of a taxi to take us to our hotel. Even though we both had to take a great deal of French when we were in school, it did not prepare us for the fast pace of the actual spoken language coming at our tired ears. It's important to remember this was before cellular phones with pocket-sized maps. Our faith and fumbled French led us to the hotel our co-worker recommended.

We unpacked our well-stuffed bags before falling exhausted into bed. I learned for this trip that Dad is an expert packer and could get twice as much stuff into the same space as I could. You've both inherited or learned from his mad clothing folding skills.

On our first day in Paris, we did the top touristy thing to do. We grabbed our fanny packs, turned to the front to keep our passports safe and cash ready, and walked to climb the Eiffel Tower. En route, we passed the American Embassy, heavily guarded by men with machine guns. We made jokes about Americans, their love of guns, and their misplaced sense of importance.

It was at the base of the Eiffel Tower that I began a frustrating relationship with toilets in Europe. You had to pay to pee and I, for a reason unknown to me yet, had begun to pee at a rate far higher than any I had experienced in my life. I thought maybe it was the nerves of traveling to a new place, but the urgency is what had me confused.

We found our way to the top of the tower, where we took our first picture with you, my firstborn son. It's the one you've seen of an unrecognizable young version of your dear parents, french fries poised in our hands, obliviously smiling as the landscape of the world forever changed around us.

We were making this trek to the top of the iconic Eiffel Tower on September 11, 2001. Those heavily armed guards were standing watch as planes crashed into the Twin Towers in New York City. And the space my bladder had previously inhabited was shrinking due to my growing uterus, which would be your home for the coming nine months.

Dad really wanted me to take a pregnancy test in Paris.

He stood outside a pharmacy saying, "Come on, wouldn't that be such a great story?" My hormone-flooded body only wanted to get to the airport and begin our trek back home. We had been gone over seventeen days of news broadcasts about terrorists and coming attacks. I'd packed and unpacked tampons at every stop and my damned hair was doing some wild thing that left it limp and unresponsive on my head. Food was no longer appealing; I longed for the comfort of a country whose rules I knew and trusted. I wasn't up for another uncomfortable interaction of partial words and animated arms. I refused. True to form, this did not dampen your father's spirit. Instead, he broke into song in the streets of Paris chanting, "You're pregnant," over and over until I broke into a smile and a tiny part of my mind relaxed.

It was upon our return to Vancouver Island that I took a pregnancy test that quickly confirmed what Dad had been declaring in the streets of Paris—I was pregnant. This was the same day I started a brand-new job as a preschool teacher. Walking out the door for the first time knowing you were growing in my womb, I felt a sense of concern. It was like I was tending to something so fragile that I already loved, and I really did not know how to keep you safe.

With you, my second born, I had taken a couple of pregnancy tests before the one that announced your arrival. We had decided to have another baby, but I was still breastfeeding and not really paying much attention to my menstrual cycle while chasing a super-active toddler. I was off the mark a couple of times, which led to the mistaken pregnancy tests. I vividly remember the day I got it right, though.

We were living on Cedar Hill. I'd left you, my firstborn, at home playing with Dad, and headed over to Zellers at the mall. It was December of 2003, and we were planning a trip up to Parksville to see Gram and Gramps for an early Christmas because we'd be spending the holidays in Brockville with Gramma D. and Gump. Returning home, pregnancy test in a plastic bag, I climbed the cement steps toward the white beveled door of our home. As my right arm reached for the doorknob I knew my life would be forever altered the next time I walked out of that door.

Locked behind the bathroom door, I heard you, my firstborn, singing on the other side while I peed on the stick and waited to see the truth of your existence, my second born, present itself. It's worth chuckling at the part of the story where we handed the same stick to your Gram and Gramps to announce your arrival, and they both looked confused by what it was. It was lost on me that pregnancy tests were not a thing when the two of them were having children.

The second time around, I knew I was capable of keeping you safe and was able to move about with a confidence that was missing during my first pregnancy. That may be true about the entire journey as a mother, the first time around versus the second time. All of this to tell you both, the moment those pregnancy tests confirmed your existences, I was in love and ready to protect you.

Yours the moment the pee stick turned positive,
Mama

EMBRACING MOTHERHOOD

Hello My Loves,

So often when you watch the Hollywood versions of parenting you see a woman effortlessly slip into the role of tending to their newborn human. In fact, before meeting the two of you, I truly did believe that this was how I was going to become your mother. I mean, it was what I wanted, and I had the body parts required to both birth and feed you. So, I thought that once you arrived, there would be a part of me turned on that knew how to be your mother.

Prior to becoming your mother, I had been a babysitter, camp counselor, daycare provider, preschool teacher, elementary school teacher, and recreation facilitator with two separate degrees in how to care for children, so I thought those things might give me a head start. I knew going in that my work experience would not directly transfer to parenting—I knew the two were different. Yet, I thought it did set me up to have some sort of advantage in terms of how to understand young humans.

I'll never forget, and trust you've heard this story more than once, the bath I took after giving birth. I think it was close to forty-eight hours into my role as a mother. Exhausted, I lay back on the cold porcelain tub begging the warm water to soothe the aching parts of my body, once so familiar and now foreign. My mind drifted to counting the days until I would rest from the weight of working. I had been using this technique to escape exhaustion for years. I would count forward to the weekend when I would have time to rest, recover, and do some of the things I loved to do. My breath caught in my throat as I realized there was no end— no days off to count toward. I had begun the sort of work that would last a lifetime. I sobbed, deep and primal, for a loss I had not expected—the loss of who I was the moment before you arrived.

It's not that I didn't love you or that I wasn't up for the work. I was simply underprepared for the grief. Yes, you read that right: the grief. No one told me that when I became your mother, the moment you left my womb and landed in my arms, I would have to say goodbye to the person I was the moment before. The carefree days of lounging about, dreaming only of my wants and needs, were gone. Because at that moment, I knew I would again meet days of lounging and rest, but they would always have your well-being at the edges of my mind. I would forever have a piece of my body wandering around outside of me. And not any old piece of my body—the piece that I valued higher than myself. The sort of carefree life one knows before inviting this worry into the world is what those sobs of mine tried to gather in the bathtub moment that began the journey of joy and grief so many call motherhood.

Without regrets,
Mama

WHAT I LOVE ABOUT BEING YOUR MOM

Hello My Loves,

"What do you love about being a parent?" I've asked this question of others before. For all the days ahead, I am going to write my answer to that question for you.

It is the chance to witness human beings, whom I love with an unconditionality I had not known before, experience the world as their fully unique selves.

The world around me tried to confuse me into thinking that there was one right way to love you, to raise you, to impart my will upon you. Yet, from the day I met both of you, I was struck by your uniqueness and your commitment to keeping your sense of identity intact.

You, my firstborn, were exposed to more experiments in mothering than you, my second born, were. At the same time, you, my firstborn, were the one who broke the mold inside of me that was looking for the one "right" way to be a mother. I am beyond grateful for the patience you showed me as a first-time mom.

Not once did you retract your love or threaten to leave me. Instead, you showed me how to best love you. In each of your protests, cries, and declarations, there was an invitation to learn how to be a better version of myself.

There are a number of places in the world where I have written about your birth, the first lesson in trust you ever taught me, so I won't repeat it all on these pages. I wonder though if it was the freedom we experienced to listen to each other without interference in that moment that set us up for all the moments that came after. It was a big job, to come into the world out of the safe place you had been nestled for so long. Your tiny fist pressed next to your cheek, landing in dad's hands to give your first cry, changing absolutely everything I knew about the world and how to be in it.

I've been asked more than once how we started on the less-than-conventional path of learning at home together. I don't have a straight answer. Yet, here as I write this letter to you, I wonder if it started with that decision to birth you at home. It was an unconventional entrance that gave us the freedom to know each other differently from that first breath.

I know there is a part of me that died the moment you were born, a carefree existence I would never again know. There was also a part of me that was born at that moment—a part that somehow knew you had arrived to be one of my greatest teachers. I didn't have the words for it then, but I will forever be grateful for the parts of you that showed up so unabashedly committed to your sense of self. I could see my only option was to learn from you and unlearn from a world that had misled me.

I can still see that time, those early years, with a vividness not all my memories hold. The plastic vines stapled to the ceiling to make the appearance of looking up from the jungle floor. The view out the French doors to our top floor balcony at the head of the Galloping Goose Trail that ran into town. I see the view, propped up on my side while feeding you. I learned how to breastfeed lying down, and since it was something the two of us struggled with, I was best at it when I was lying down next to your tiny self. We spent hours like that in the beginning. I decided every woman was better at mothering than I was, as they walked by—hair washed, clothes cleaned, with a joyful baby tucked under a blanket inside the stroller. I still didn't know how to wash myself and my clothing on the same day, always dirty in body or outfit. I wouldn't dare walk out the front door for fear you would scream for food and there would be nowhere to lie down. On the first few walks we took, you screamed in the stroller, so I gave up even trying to bring it.

From the wide-angle view I now have, that is the moment when I began to recognize your teachings—there truly was no one "right" way to do things. I was a somewhat unclean mama lying in bed to nurse, who carried her baby outside of the stroller in order to meet him exactly where he was. Your happiness began to take center stage, letting judgment (on my good days) fall to the sidelines.

It would be easy for me, all these years later, to tell you that I dropped that judgment and jumped into showing up for you. That would be a disservice to you, should you ever enter2 the world of parenting, and to anyone else who might read these pages. Separating from what you know and entering a different way of being in the world takes a courage that was only just beginning to grow inside of me.

I knew somehow, that if I pushed my agenda upon you, it would break something inside of you that I had only just begun to understand; it seemed like a terrible idea to miss out on the chance of knowing that part better. So, I boldly asked friends if I could lay in their beds when I visited so you could get the kind of feeding that came when we were both relaxed. I pushed the stroller out of the way and wrapped you in a sling, and I found hats to hide my nest of hair for however many days it took to wash it. We were falling in love, deeply in love, and it was going to require both courage and action for me to get it right.

You, my second born, shot into this world like a cannon. It was a much different birth since I had your older brother dancing around wondering what was going on. It is fascinating to see the difference doing something for the first time and doing it over again. I walked in with bolstered-up courage that had me thinking I knew what I was doing. Yet, like every human being, each birth is unique. You arrived on your due date (despite my best efforts to will you to arrive earlier), with speed, in the early evening. Contractions started after I did a full grocery shop—loading all the bags in the car myself even though Dad made me promise I would ask for help—and snuggled your brother into a nap. Finally laying down for my own nap, I realized you were on your way.

When your brother was born, I had a chorus of people encouraging me with updates on the progress of his emerging head. With you, attention was pulled in different directions, so I had to call out, "Can anyone see the head?" With affirmations that you were right there, I went into a deep squat and pushed you out into my arms. Falling back, I announced, "It's a boy, and I am never doing that again!" The speed and intensity of your arrival set the tone for our learning journey.

Where your brother struggled to gain weight, you impressed everyone with the ounces you immediately began gaining. Where he was awake in the morning, you were awake in the evening. You see, I was under the pretense that I knew how to be a mother, so I would be ready for whatever it was you brought along. Truthfully, what the past two years had taught me was that I knew how to be your brother's mother, and you had arrived to teach me how to be yours. And though it would require the same attention and unconditional love, the nuances and the "how" would be purely unique to you.

Plus, there was a lesson, the falling of grace, that I was not prepared for. I had been the mom who was there the second my child cried, now I was outnumbered and I was going to have to learn how to share the load and be okay with you crying just a little longer while I juggled both of your needs.

With honor and grace,
Mama

BABIES DON'T COME
WITH MANUALS

Hello My Loves,

In case you have not learned this on your own yet, I want to let you know that babies do not come with manuals. You know, like all the other important things you buy, start out with, or are hired to do, that generally come with a few instructions on how to, at the very least, get started. Again, babies, the most vulnerable things that you are in charge of keeping alive, do not come with an instruction manual.

You, my firstborn, on the midwife's first post-visit checkup, were weighed wearing a cloth diaper. It put you closer to your birth weight than you would have been if you were weighed in all your nakedness. I share this because it kicked off a series of terrible moments that had me wishing there was a manual for the care and feeding of newborn humans. I don't mean the sort of books that exist that are written by overeducated men who have never had their insides brought outside and then were tasked with using their bodies to keep something alive.

When the midwife returned two day later and weighed you again, the diaper was off, so you appeared to be losing weight at a rate that suggested you weren't actually eating enough to thrive. Add this to me, your mother, who had not slept for a full night in weeks with brand new emotions, and you begin to get a sense of the urgency that erupted from the pit of my stomach—robbing me of any sense of reason I might have been holding on to. I was certain she said to me, "You are failing as a mother. Your child is not thriving because of your incompetence."

I would also like to warn you that there is a thing called "evening colic" that can show up in babies at the same moment that their desperate mothers are trying to get enough breast milk into them to ensure they gain the appropriate amount of weight to thrive. Every single day of your infancy, just before Dad would get home from work, you, my firstborn, would begin to cry. Not little boo-hoos, they were full-on desperate-and-inconsolable-body-thrusting cries. I was certain it was because you were starving to death, so I would spend the moments until Dad got home trying to get you to nurse. The more frantic I was, the more frantic you were.

Dad would walk in the door, and I would hand you to him while you were screaming. The thing is, though, that it was really hard for me to listen to you cry. So, it's not like I handed you off, put my feet up and relaxed. I would hand you off, sit nervously on the edge of my seat, and critique everything Dad tried to do. Once a health nurse explained to us this thing called "evening colic" and showed us how much a cloth diaper can weigh, we were able to come up with a plan that would allow me to potentially have thirty minutes of relaxation on those challenging evenings.

Dad would come in the door, I would hand you off if you were screaming, then he would do something for fifteen minutes before handing you back. There was the football hold, where he had your tiny limbs hanging from his forearm, face down, in hopes this change of positioning would help. There was also the sway in front of the bathroom mirror with the water running, rocking in the rocking chair, placing the car seat on the dryer, and running the vacuum, to name a few. If you calmed down at all, you remained in whoever's arms you were in. They continued doing what they were doing until you started to scream again. If you didn't calm down, whoever was holding you knew that they only had to make it fifteen minutes before they could take a break. Even thinking back to it now all these lifetimes later, my heartbeat rises. There is nothing more desperate than the feeling that you cannot console your child who is screaming as though the world is ending.

But we made it through. The kind health nurse we met let us know that around the six-week mark things would settle down. Well, they would settle down in terms of the night-time scream fest—there would be new things to send our fresh parenting selves into a chaotic panic.

Now, when you came along, my second born, we thought for sure we knew a few things about being parents. I mean, we had been doing it for a full two years and had successfully kept your brother alive, so for sure we were going to be ready for you. I can laugh now. I was not laughing back then when you came out of the gates with a fiery personality, unlike your brother's. It was within hours of being born that you taught us a baby can cry more than just through the evening hours. A baby can arrive in the world, ready to gain weight, and still scream at his parents for reasons no one could begin to solve.

I haven't done the research, but I am certain there must be some sort of memory-erasing hormone released into young parents' minds that allows them to agree to have another child. Because unlike your brother, you were ready for the nightly scream fests from day one. There was no lead-up to it, no rhyme, no reason, and no predictability. I was there holding you with the same level of uncertainty I had when managing your brother's screaming.

The newness, the freshness . . . I could never have predicted the second time around. You would scream during the exact moments that your big brother would want me to help him out, and it was always at his bedtime. Giving me, a freshly minted mother of two, the most impossible choice of picking which screaming child to tend to. I was thrown into the trenches of choosing who got my attention.

I sat, tears streaming down my face in the gold fabric rocking chair, with my newborn wailing for attention while my toddler, nestled in Dad's arms, screamed, "Mama! I want my mama!" The bile in my stomach churns even as I write these words, and the memory of it all races into my body. It's truly impossible to choose, and that was the moment I realized it would never be possible to be everything for the both of you all the time.

Like the bathtub episode I mentioned earlier, this was the moment when I began to mourn the mother I had been before you, my second treasure, arrived in the world. You see, I had the chance to develop a sense, a definition, and an identity as a good mother. I was there for each whim, worry, and whimper with the solution, or at the very least the console of my arms. Now I was staring down the reality that there would be a lifetime of whims, worries, and woes that I would never be able to tend to for the both of you. My entire identity as a mother shattered there on the living room floor as I wept, listening to the cries of two children begging for the sole attention of one mother.

Picking up the pieces of that shattered identity, I knew that unconditional love would be the glue that held us together and brought us back to one another. No one person can possibly be everything to another. We can, however, agree to do everything we need to tend to our relationship.

Yours, heart split in two,
Mama

FREEDOM FROM THE
BODY POLICE

Hello My Loves,

We are not living in a world that encourages people to trust their bodies. I would say quite the opposite is happening, especially for women. Now I know the two of you (my sons) are not women, but you will live alongside them in the world and should be aware that there is a lot of policing of women's bodies that goes on. In fact, there is actually a lot of policing of bodies that happens in the world in general.

We are told what to eat, what is an acceptable weight, how we should move our bodies, and on and on it goes. As a parent, I also think it is true that we are trained to believe we are somehow in charge of our children's bodies. Well-meaning advice tells parents, we are supposed to make you sleep on a schedule that is determined by us, and to feed you on a schedule that is determined by us.

I wish I could reach back in time and share with you the exact moment I learned to trust you and your bodies. I know it was early on and likely tied to on-demand breastfeeding. You, my firstborn, took a little longer to start gaining weight in the way that those watching wanted you to, so there was all this watching and waiting and measuring that had me losing sight of you. I remember when I called for support, bereft and certain I was doing everything wrong, and that those actions, at any moment in time, could lead to your death. The woman on the other end of the call saved us both. She very matter-of-factly told me to get into bed with you, skin to skin, and stay there for twenty-four to seventy-two hours. It was so simple. It did not involve the machine we had rented to attach to my breasts to try and encourage them to pump out more milk, or the plastic bottles we placed the minuscule amounts of breast milk in that you absolutely rejected having anywhere near your mouth. It was you and me, side by side, trying to figure our way through what I now believe was someone else's idea of a problem between us. The results were almost immediate, as my milk started to come in more fully and your weight started to slowly inch its way up.

You, my second born, also had some troubles when entering this big world. You kicked butt at gaining weight, partly due to the fact that you weren't actually pooping at all. That's a story we have laughed at over and over. I was not concerned until day ten when the midwives started to wonder. I will never forget the look on your newborn face when we inserted the suppository that unleashed what can only be referred to as a soft serve ice cream tap wide open. Dad had tears streaming down his face as he grabbed diaper after diaper in an attempt to help me collect ten days' worth of newborn poop. That was our first sign your digestive system was going to need a whole different kind of attention. In the beginning, it looked like it was all tied to a dairy allergy, but as time went on, I suspected more and more that it was gluten since I had issues with gluten myself.

Here is where our path diverged from what others might have done. I was already gluten-free, so much of what we ate fell into that category. I wasn't going to police what you ate, though. I was not living in your body. So, when you decided to eat something with gluten in it, I would bite my tongue and hold my breath. I also slept with a barf bowl under my bed and was ready to capture vomit from any meal gone wrong while out in public. I would reflect back to you what you had eaten and what the results had been. Many times, you would commit to not eating gluten, and then fall off the wagon at the offer of a delicious sub.

I want to pause here for someone who might be reading and thinking I was being an abusive parent for letting you eat something you may have had an allergy to. We had in fact taken you for allergy testing.. The screening presented that you had a nut allergy, and knowing that information yourself, you chose to never eat nuts. When consulting about testing for a gluten allergy, our doctor said you'd need to eat a full gluten diet for a couple of months to get an accurate diagnosis, but he would not recommend that if there was already evidence of discomfort.

You would try your darndest for weeks on end to not eat gluten, and then a delicious treat would show up and tempt you to go all in. There was not always vomiting immediately after the fact, so it was hard for you to tie the two together at your young age. Then July 21, 2013, came. We were at Maggiano's on Santana Row, and you were all over the bread and breaded chicken breasts before, wide-eyed, you looked at me and said, "Take me to the bathroom." There was a violence in your projectile vomiting that I had not seen before. Once the contents of your stomach were in the toilet, you turned to me with puffy eyes and announced, "I am never eating gluten again." And you stayed true to that promise.

As time went by and you settled into your new stomach, you shared with me what you began to notice. You shared that you would eat so little of your meals at times because you thought you were full when, in fact, you were bloated. You would feel hungry again so quickly after eating. That explained all those "surprise" snacks I had to make for you. The first time I saw you complete an entire burger and side of fries was when you ate an In and Out burger wrapped in lettuce. You settled back into your body and were able to hear what it was telling you.

I share these stories as examples of the power of listening to your body, knowing what it needs and wants, and nourishing yourself from that place. It is true that sometimes, like in the above examples, you have to make all the wrong decisions first in order to find the one right solution that works for the body you are living in. The challenge for me as your mom has always been trying to let go of my own stories and inside voices in order to support you in listening to yours. I had never lived inside your body, but I only tried to be the best alongside-you support I could be.

Yours in gluten-free glory,

Mama

PARENTING IS WHO I AM

Hello My Loves,

On one of our many road trips, I fired up Shonda Rhimes's *Year of Yes* audiobook on the stereo. Partway through the book, she shares how she came to see parenting not as a job but as who she was. I immediately grabbed a recording device and started talking through this big idea. I had referred to parenting as a job on more than one occasion. This new idea of hers gave me pause for some serious reflection.

For many people, a job is something that one regularly wants a break from. It's laborious. It can suck from time to time. There is compensation for time and effort and there can be overtime. But often there are complaints about hours and even sleepless nights. Co-workers can point out issues you would rather not deal with. There may be chances for bonuses, and a certain level of knowledge is required to succeed in most cases. Writing these examples down, I can most certainly draw some parallels between parenting and the workforce. I can understand how we, as a society, have come to consider parenting a job. However, jobs are often something we have to get through, struggle with, or do when we'd rather not.

Alternatively, if I start to ask questions about who I am, the words that flow forward have a much more positive spin on them.

I am kind, thoughtful, hardworking, considerate, loving, and the list goes on. The energy I bring to considering who I am as opposed to what job I do comes from a place much more grounded in the impact I hope to have on the world around me. It strips me back to my fundamental character and considers the values I hold dear.

When I turn this all back around to parenting, I find myself nodding enthusiastically alongside Shonda. Yes, parenting is who I am. It is not what I do. It is who I am because it is wrapped up in my heart. It's an action and response that comes from my core values. It is how I tend to the most fragile parts of who I am. This is not to say it isn't challenging, exhausting, or frustrating at times. It instead defines what I hold onto in those most desperate moments to pick me up again to meet myself with compassion in order to bring my best self forward.

Turning toward parenting as who I am, not a job I do, affords me the freedom to be my best self at each turn of the journey. Responding to struggle with love, I want to be known as someone who can do hard things, especially the ones outside my comfort zone. Choosing kindness, I want to be a trusted resource to those who are vulnerable. Providing compassion, I know at the heart of who I am that I want to be someone who offers a hand up, not a push down. I want to apply curiosity to all the situations that arise because I want to be known as someone who can think way outside of the box to uncover a solution that no one else considered—one that lifts each person to their highest potential—persevering in the face of adversity over and over again to raise a stronger human being. Honestly connecting with the humans in front of me, I want to find the space between us that is our shared humanity. This list of who I am, is the parent I become when I see this one piece of my journey as an extension of who I am and not a job I must do.

Yours as mother,

Mama

DITCHING DIAPERS

Hello My Loves,

I will forever remember the moment I was sitting in the hallway outside the bathroom of our home just up the road from the park. You, my second born, were squirming under my diaper change while I had one eye on the pages of the book, *The Kite Runner,* that I simply could not put down, and the other on you, my firstborn, as I begged you to poop in the potty. I was offering up at the time what was your most prized possession: a full-sized red Freezie. I had changed at least three poopy diapers that day, so the last thing I wanted was another of your four-year-old, gigantic poops while we were at the park.

You sat there, tiny legs dangling from the toilet seat, doing everything you could to make your body do something it just did not want to do. You started to sob when the words, "I'll buy you a big red Freezie" left my mouth. Snapping back to reality, I looked at you, doing everything you possibly could to make me happy and earn the magical reward. I, too, started to sob. You were not trying, in any way, to make my life more challenging. You were just being a little boy ready to go and play in the park with his mom and brother. Finishing the diaper change in front of me, I picked you up off the potty and begged you to stop sobbing. I offered you two Freezies while apologizing over and over again for my misstep. You know this story better than I do, as you tell it again and again as one of those moments when your mom really messed up the whole parenting thing.

You see, in the early years, I was super influenced by the way others were doing things and less in touch with what you needed from me as a mom. Parenting books and forums told me you should be using the toilet at this particular stage in your life, so I tried to force the issue. This far out from it all, I can assure you each child comes to potty training at their own rate. There is no hard and fast rule that will work for every child. The best way to avoid making your young child cry is to check in with them every step of the way and meet them where they are at.

I would love to say this is the day that I learned this lesson and that was it because we blissfully continued together, never again bumping into potty training issues. But that would be a lie. Somewhere along the way, I saw a commercial, ironically enough probably from a diaper company, encouraging positive potty training for parents and children. The idea was that you let your child know that as soon as they pooped on the potty there was to be a party in their honor. Now, what the commercial failed to recognize is that young children and adults don't always understand the world in the same way.

The next time you were willing to hop up on the toilet to try pooping in it, I announced, "We will have an I-pooped-in-the-potty party as soon as you poop." It all seemed innocent enough in the moment. You, however, elected to return to your pull-up for many more months. Years later, when we were reminiscing about these challenging moments, you shared that you had understood my party invitation to be that all of us, your friends included, would crowd around you in the bathroom while you pooped. This sounds horrible and makes absolute sense as to why you wanted no part of that.

All of this to say to you, my dear sons, that should you ever find yourself having or being in the company of children, it is most effective to meet them where they are at, listen to them, and make darn sure you share an understanding of what a particular event requires. It's okay to ask too many times to ensure you are both on the same page.

Yours in hilarity,
Mama

MUSICAL BEDS

Hello My Loves,

It has been fascinating to share conversations with you over the years, understanding how our musical-bed-sharing sleep situations were experienced by you. There was a moment when we were watching the show *Lost,* and the character Kate ran down the hall toward a three-year-old child crying in the night. You, my firstborn said, "Yeah right, as if anyone sleeps that far away from their child." It was that moment that I realized you thought our sleeping ways were the norm. Through the years, you have come to understand that parenting is unique to each family, and it has broadened what you know. I still love that story because it showed you noticed we prioritized closeness when it came to sleep time.

I think I have mentioned already how I had ideas about sleeping before meeting the two of you. Dad and I invested what little time and money we had in creating the perfect jungle room for you to rest in, my firstborn. Nani and I spent an entire day assembling the crib that Gramps so proudly purchased for you. Then reality set in. I met you and could not imagine having you anywhere but right next to me. Even if I could have done it, in those early months, you were not sleeping anywhere that did not involve my warm body.

I spent a lot of time reading and learning about sleep and what might bring it on when I first became a mother. If you do a quick Google search, you will get a sense of how vast this topic is and how varied the opinions are. The truth for me was that I loved to sleep, and I had been really great at it until I gave birth and had to keep a tiny human alive. Everything changed and all I wanted was those hours back. The advice most commonly given to new mothers is to "sleep when the baby sleeps" without ever explaining how the heck showering, cooking, and cleaning happens if the two of you are sleeping at the same time. So, I was all kinds of mixed up in the beginning, trying to find a book that would fix a problem I thought I had.

Sleep might be the place where our journey began to veer off the mainstream course. I learned to nurse lying down, as it was the easiest for both of us. It made sense that we slept together. Why would I get out of bed to grab you, lie down and nurse you, and then move both of us back to our separate beds? That seemed like a waste of a lot of good lying-down-potentially-sleeping moments. So, we slept side by side, and I nursed you half-awake and half-asleep throughout the night. Then when your night wakings got in the way of Dad resting before going to work, I moved into a bed next to you in that beautiful jungle room with the crib-turned-toy-storage bin. The goal was always for each of us to get as much sleep as possible, no matter what that looked like or what people who did not know us thought about how we were doing things.

As the years went on, this was our approach to sleeping, doing whatever configuration brought about the most restful nights for each person. This meant recording "pretend stories" for you to listen to, my second born, when I simply could not keep my eyes open as long as you could. Then came the purchase of a bigger bed so Dad could sleep all through the night with you, my firstborn, when the world was too topsy-turvy for you to rest without his presence. There were bunk beds assembled and taken apart, middle of the night tip toes from one bed to another, calls out for me to return, and countless sweet memories of hilarious lessons learned in the conversations that unfolded as the four of us nestled side by side, waiting for some form of sleep to arrive.

I share this with you to remind you that, in some moments, it's best to turn toward those humans you adore and listen to what their hearts are telling you they need. It might appear strange to someone looking in from the outside, but I assure you that you'll forget those strange looks and hold on to the sweet loving memories.

Finally sleeping through the night again,
Mama

YOU CANNOT SPOIL A CHILD
WITH LOVE AND ATTENTION

Hello My Loves,

The world around us does not regularly offer support for meeting our child's needs on a regular or immediate basis. Honestly, it might stretch in the opposite direction, somehow convincing us that interacting with our children over and over again in a way that meets their needs is somehow spoiling them. But for something to spoil, to turn truly rotten, it needs to be neglected. Just think of that piece of fruit rolled under the back seat of the car, unattended for days on end, and you'll understand what I am getting at. Things that are showered with love and affection do not become spoiled; they grow, in both strength and understanding of love and compassion.

This idea is not something that I was raised under. In fact, I would say my parents fell prey to a world that convinced them that loving me in a fully attentive way might spoil me. It begs the question of course, as to what it means to be a spoiled child. I notice it is more harmful to ignore or neglect something than to fall head over heels in love with it.

It's true that before I met you, I might have thought you could spoil a child by meeting their every need. I think it comes from the idea that a child who gets whatever they want will just keep asking for things. A fear, perhaps, of gluttony or greed, which if you were to ever read the Bible, you would see were deadly sins. Your grandfather was raised in the Catholic Church with punitive nuns, so that could be a piece of why it is that he was certain a child needed a little bit of neglect in order to rise up into the world with a good heart or something of the sort.

There is also this common myth that babies manipulate their parents right from the get-go, which is such an odd idea to me. If you study Maslow's hierarchy of needs or read anything about child development, you will see on your own that babies do not have the skill set or even a brain developed enough to "manipulate" through guilt. A baby comes into the world and is simply trying to get its basic needs met. If they are met, the baby is content; if they are not met, the baby is not content.

You can read all kinds of theories about sleep and sleep training, some of which spring from the idea of both spoiling and manipulating. As you read earlier, I really believed upon meeting you, my firstborn, that I would place you in your crib and you would peacefully drift off to sleep when you were tired. This was not what happened. In an attempt to get us both as much sleep as possible, we slept close to each other, in the same bed, so that I did not have to get up every time you wanted to eat. It truly was the best way to provide each of us with what we needed. I remember lying on the futon one particular night, looking up at the ceiling, and feeling a little frustrated by your desire to have me close by for sleep to happen. Questioning if the books were actually right about leaving you alone in this dark room to cry until you exhausted yourself to sleep, it hit me that you and I had been in the same body for nine months. How in the world were you going to just naturally fall asleep with me being a whole room away? This is the stuff I think our world forgets to think about. It is focused on its self-centeredness and never once stops to think things through your lens. That is a gift I have had for many parts of my life—the ability to see the world through the eyes of a child. And it is this gift that helped me have patience for your need to have me nearby.

You both will make whatever decisions feel right in partnership with any human you choose to create life with. My one and only wish would be that you consider the tiny human in front of you as you make each of your decisions, choosing partnership over power and relationship over rules. That being said, I will love you through it all.

Yours in spoiling,
Mama

TRUSTING YOU FROM THE BEGINNING

Hello My Loves,

When you were both babies, I upset a number of people by not letting them hold you. At first, I thought I was perhaps being selfish by wanting to keep you all to myself. Maybe I was somehow weak because I was incapable of sitting calmly nearby when you were using your only communication device, crying, to let the world know you were unhappy. It wasn't enough for me to wait for the other person to catch up and attempt to soothe you when I knew my arms could do that faster than anyone else.

This is not to say I was some sort of martyr who had to be the one to calm you down. I simply noticed that I was the one who had the most experience hearing what it was you were asking for. Often, you just wanted to be held close to the one you felt the safest with. The world is a big place full of noises, smells, and sounds that can be confusing to newly arrived human beings. So, I took the cold looks and sarcastic comments on the chin and scooped you inside my arms to help you understand the world. Those who stayed around long enough came to see it was worth the wait. If they were willing to still engage lovingly with you in my arms, they would soon be invited into the circle of trusted humans. Also, if you returned to my arms when you asked, you were much faster to visit their arms again.

It was about respect and consent. This is not something people talk about when it comes to babies. Most of the books and message boards I visited at the time talked about methods that involved ignoring you or letting you cry to a place of self-soothing. These all seemed to go against what my heart was calling out for, which was to meet you right where you were in the moment and help you meet those needs.

I was raised under the idea that respect was something that you either earned or gave to someone who had been alive longer than you. I was always, even as a small child, confused by the idea that if someone was being mean or rude to me, I had to be nice to them because they had been alive for more years than I had. If I could figure out that their behavior was bad, why couldn't they? So together, Dad and I made the decision that we would respect the two of you simply because you were alive. We weren't going to make you earn anything. We decided to create you, you arrived, and that alone was enough. This goes at the top of the list of good decisions we've made as your parents.

Through respecting you as humans, we were able to put meeting your needs on the same level as meeting our own. It was uncommon to do this in the world we were living in at the time. I did not have any experience with this at all. In fact, the opposite could be said to be true. I had gone through twelve years of school, five years of university, and then entered into working in systems that simply did not respect or value children as equals. We were still pulling ourselves out of the children-should-be-seen-and-not-heard generation, but as I mentioned above, I had known this to be wrong my entire life.

The first babysitting job I had was with a little boy who had cerebral palsy. I was twelve years old, and I was the one his parents trusted most to stay with him and his younger sister, mostly because I could get him to do the things other childcare providers simply could not. Do you know how I did it? I listened to him. I gave him what I longed for as a child—the room to express himself and be a part of solutions. I wish I could tell you where I learned this skill, but when I look back, it simply seemed to be built into the fiber of who I was. This is not to say this can't be learned or taught. I was lucky enough to know it on a cellular level early on in my years working side by side with younger humans.

Through all the years, the jobs, and the trainings, I was always most drawn to children who had trouble being seen and understood by the humans around them. I was known in the field for being able to support "challenging" children in "fitting in." Again, my secret was not to make them fit in at all. It was to witness them, listen to them, and work with them so they could have a most enjoyable experience. Contrary to popular belief, children do not want to cause trouble. They are hardwired to please; some of them just need a little help translating what that looks like in various situations. And the adults around them need a **lot** of practice in both listening and translating.

Even with all these years of training and experience under my belt, the two of you taught me many new things. You were skilled in locating my trigger points, and you had my heart in ways no other children I had met ever could. It was this unconditional love and my commitment that guided me to meet you just where you were, listen outside of my wounds, and partner together to find ways forward that respected each one of us.

Yours in respect,
Mama

A STYLE OF YOUR OWN

Hello My Loves,

As you know, I was brought up in a mainstream school system and even went on to learn how to be a teacher within that system. After seventeen years of schooling and another five years working in that system, I decided not to send you into the same system. I had begun deconstructing what I knew about learning before I met the two of you, but I give most of the credit for what I now know directly to the two of you.

Learning never happens in a straight line. I know the school system wants us to believe that it does because all their funding relies on it. But I know without a doubt from years of learning with you, watching Dad, and eventually through letting go and following my own interests that learning is a wild ride in all kinds of directions. When you were first learning to read, my second born, you blew my mind wide open. We were standing at the park with the wooden train in Santa Clara. I had my new bike with me, and its seat had the word "demo" written on it. You looked over and said, "Hey, that's the first letter of 'dad,' the last letter of 'the'" and the first two letters of 'mom.'" You could not tell me what the letters were called, but you were already reading. That is one of the moments when I felt strongly we were on the right learning path. You had the freedom to find a system of reading that matched your individual learning style, and it did not look like anything I had seen in my twenty-plus years in the mainstream school system.

I share this not to say the mainstream school system is a bad thing—it serves a purpose—but to highlight the strength that comes from leaning into your own learning style and letting that be what guides you toward new information.

Countless times, I have seen the two of you dive deep into an interest until it ran out and walked away, then years later pick up exactly where you left off and add another layer to the interest. Take hockey, for example. That was something you, my firstborn, immersed in off-ice for four years before lacing up and hitting the ice, where you were able to catch up to your peers at an impressive speed. Then, you put it down again for three years. Later, you returned with such determination that you were placed at the highest division you qualified for.

Time and time again, you both teach me that value lies in the trust you have in your own ability to learn. It is a motivation that comes from within when the time is right, and the information is present. I am grateful for how I have been able to use this lesson to rebuild my own trust in my ability to learn whatever tugs at my heart.

Yours in learning,
Mama

LEARNING DOESN'T HAPPEN IN A STRAIGHT LINE

Hello My Loves,

Here is something I suspect you already know: learning does not always occur in a straight line or logical order. This was hard for me when I became a mother.

The first place I learned about this was in the department of sleep. The moment one of you slept for a coveted number of hours, I was certain this was a new skill you would use every single day. You can stop laughing now. Sleep, as I wrote about a few letters earlier, always happened and rarely looked like I thought it would.

Often, when young children are learning a new skill or passing a milestone, they regress in other areas. I saw this when the two of you were in your respective baby and toddler years. You would master walking, then be up half the night needing to nurse more often as you tried to figure out the new world you were living in. You would gather the courage to spend an hour away from me with your grandparents, then need me to sit beside you for the rest of the day. Launching out into the bigger world and gathering new skills takes time to integrate into the depths of knowledge. This is why you often needed more of my time or attention while these new things made their way fully into your understanding of the world.

When you were eight years old, my firstborn, after years of successfully sleeping on your own after fall-asleep cuddles with Dad, it became impossible for him to slip out of the room. You needed him next to you. When I look back now, I see how it ties into that time in your growth when you were stepping outside of egocentrism toward a wider understanding of the world around you. Ideas became realities and your mind was having a difficult time accepting that hard things weren't just ideas but true realities for humans. That can be a lot for a mind to wrap itself around. The art for us as your parents has always been to meet you exactly where you are and grow from there, as opposed to dragging you kicking and screaming to where our adult selves thought you should be.

You, my second born, had a similar experience when you were unable to exist in the world without me nearby early in your ninth year of life. You may remember this because it coincided with one of Gram's visits. You wept for hours each day, unable to leave the house or be without having your eyes on me. You had mourned Gramp's death for almost six years, but as your understanding of the world expanded, you recognized I would never see my dad again. You couldn't imagine the weight of that or the knowledge that one day you might not be able to see my face. Once again, we pulled back to meet you exactly where you were by adjusting our schedules. We did a lot of art and repeatedly watched the safest shows so we could predict what was going to appear on the screen. Like all the things that challenge us, this did pass, and you returned to being your vibrant, outgoing self.

Now I look back on these moments and view them as periods when you were able to grow your compassion muscles. You have both been thoughtful, caring humans from the get-go, and there have been distinct moments in your lives when I saw compassion blossom outside of you. My role was to create a safe container for it all to happen within—to sit with my feelings of discomfort and grow with you at your pace. If I had rushed you or crushed you in those moments, I would have gotten in the way of you building your compassion muscles. I think it is true in our society that children are often rushed through integrating big, new ideas into their understanding of the world. In my experience, when space is created for all the lessons to naturally make their way into your knowing, we are less likely to have to revisit them again and again. A child who is heard, respected, and valued well is likely to turn into a human who is willing to extend the same courtesy to others. To hear, respect, and value someone is a practice that is intentionally exercised. I have seen this in the two of you over and over again.

I share this handful of examples with the two of you to also help you cultivate some compassion for your growing selves. You will always be growing and bumping into ideas that you thought were well-rooted in your understanding until you discover something different, which will probably lead you to unpack things you thought you were finished with. I like to think of growing and learning as a spiral. Yes, you will encounter information, ideas, and triggers time and time again, and you might feel like you have been there before. In reality, you have stepped into a new place on the spiral and are viewing it once again with your new lived experiences. So, if you can meet yourself like I did when you were little, right where you are, not where you think you should be, and liberally apply kindness and patience, I promise you will move forward more smoothly.

Yours in constant growth,
Mama

HEARTBREAK AND GRIEF ARE INEVITABLE

Hello My Loves,

The world is a hard place. Heartbreak and grief are inevitable. I remember when I didn't believe this was true—when I was certain I could use all the joy I had inside of me to blanket your worlds with bubble wrap. I'd bend all sorts of sideways just to keep your needs met, cries caught, and worlds dripping with happiness.

My back slid down the freshly painted living room walls facing out over the ocean view. "This is how my dad dies," rang from the pit of my stomach, rendering me stuck to the floor in a pool of despair. Friends were watching you play while I figured out how to get your recently-released-from-hospital-post-hernia-surgery Dad to Parksville so that I could sit in on the doctor's report about Gramps, who'd almost had surgery the same day Dad did. They'd stopped, though, using words such as "inoperable" before returning him to his third-floor room.

No one had used the word "cancer" yet. Even though he'd fought it just four years earlier, we were deceiving ourselves with language such as "ulcerative colitis" and "intestinal obstructions." That moment on the floor, my soul overrode my mind, and I knew what was happening. It took Herculean efforts to un-know my intuition in order to pack the car with our belongings and pretend everything was ok.

I was able to get you both, then five and two, into the car with your post-op dad, half of the house, and a calm mind to make the trek up the island. I was also able to hear a doctor use words like "cancer," "inoperable," "quality of life" and "no big life decisions should be made at this time." Within two months of the diagnosis, we moved from our amazing community in Victoria to just three houses up the road from where Gramps was trying to beat his cancer.

The morning of October 16, 2007, I watched a piece of both of you disappear. You, my second son, then three years old, leaped out of bed in your pink Dora the Explorer pajamas to excitedly exclaim that you were going to take Gramps golfing with the free game you won the day before. You were meant to have spent that previous day golfing with Gramps. He had instead been admitted to the hospital for a blood transfusion, so Dad stepped in to take you on the much-anticipated mini-golf adventure. You called Gramps and told him your scores while an IV ran blood into his veins. The same blood later poured out of him as he begged me to remember how much he loved you and your brother.

The words, "Gramps died last night," fell on the carpet between us. You cried the primal tears appropriate for the loss of someone so precious to your life even without enough years to know what death really was. There's been only one other time I've heard that level of devastation pour out of you.

My firstborn, I crawled beside you on the top bunk as you pretended not to be awake. Slipping an arm under your warm body for the briefest of moments before you stirred, sat up, and met me eye to eye. It was just two days before when you looked out the church window and asked me, "Is that where we will bury Gramps when he dies?" The words locked in my throat because I did not understand how you knew what was happening when we'd been so careful with our words.

"Sweetheart, Gramps died last night." You never broke eye contact as tears blurred my vision. You also did not let a single tear out of your eyes. You nodded in recognition as something in you slipped out of sight forever.

Gramps was your biggest fan. He was the one who held you when they put your second IV in at fourteen months of age because I didn't have the courage to listen to you say, "No, Mama! No, Mama!" He was the one who drove four hours round trip to see you for one hour. He sat front row at your baptism and took you to a woodworking class at a time when you refused to leave my side. He taught you to light a fire before most would trust a child with matches. And he let you stand naked in his seat at the head of the dinner table because he knew your birth was his chance to make up for what he'd missed as a father.

The tragedy buried itself deep inside both of you and taught me that no amount of bubble wrap was going to save you from the cruel realities of an uncertain world; your hearts were made of the sort of material that rises stronger after being shattered.

Grieving with you always,
Mama

MIDDLE YEARS

Hello again, Dear Reader,

Phew! We have successfully kept these young humans alive for years now. If you are anything like me, you were hoping that all this experience might have brought a little ease into this whole parenting journey. Though it might not feel so fresh, there are still new obstacles around every corner.

In these middle years, children are growing in their confidence and voice. As they step out of such intense egocentrism, they have new questions and curiosities about the world around them. This stage in my children's lives had me once again questioning everything I thought I knew about the world and having to rewrite some outdated information in my own thinking.

My children have always been the perfect mirror of everything that made me feel uncomfortable. Once again, these letters dig into the unconditional love required to ride the inevitable highs and lows of raising young humans.

LET'S TALK ABOUT TECH, BABY

Hello My Loves,

There has been nothing easy about raising children in the age of technology that did not exist when I was growing up. You know, the olden days when I had to get off the couch to change the channel and answer the telephone that was wired into the wall. You were living with technology bursting at the seams, changing and expanding year after year.

Before I met you, I had decided that my children would watch limited amounts of TV, likely stationed on the Learning Channel, where you would sit cross-legged and wide-eyed, drinking in the knowledge being bestowed on you by an expert. I had some pretty high ideals about what sort of manipulation I would be capable of pulling off. I knew without a shadow of a doubt that the evils of video games would never land in the hands of my precious offspring because they led to smelly basement-dwelling adults who were incapable of leaving home. I had bigger plans for you. It is worth noting that Dad and I spent most evenings of our lives collapsed on the couch consuming hours of entertainment. Perhaps I had decided our brains were past the stage of saving, having rotted in front of *Sesame Street* in our youth. Oh, and Dad's spare time was often spent questing his way toward higher levels in the fictitious land in *World of Warcraft.* It's funny how early on we set out to build our children into something greater than we were even able to obtain ourselves.

I was recommitted to these issues in the dark hours of three-month-old you screaming inconsolably in my arms after that one time when Dad turned your body toward the television to see a music video, my firstborn. Google had assured me that the over-stimulation most certainly led to the first of many years' worth of night terrors. TV remained in the "evil" category.

A short three months later, I propped you in your exersaucer and turned on the television to entertain you for the first time. Parenting alone at home with a baby is the most exhausting task I have ever been up against. Dad was working twelve-hour days, and that is a lot of time to spend with a human who needs constant observation.

I'd reasoned that fifteen minutes of screen time was fine so that I could get dinner started. At that time, there was an entire channel dedicated to children's programming: TreeHouse. I was certain that somewhere behind the design of this program was an education expert. It's funny the mental gymnastics a mind can do when it is trying to hold on to its sense of rightness in the world.

Fifteen minutes slipped into thirty minutes as my exhausted self started cleaning the kitchen while making dinner. I thought if I could move frantically through the kitchen, dishwasher open, emptied, filled, I could buy myself an early collapse on the couch after your bedtime. Yes, you guessed it, to lose myself in my own television viewing.

Then we met Elmo, the first love of your life, and any sense of control I thought I had fell out the window. You were enamored, insistent, and absolutely committed to engaging with this red puppet who spoke to himself in the third person, and I was too tired to fight. It was at your second birthday party, firstborn, that someone asked us when you would stop speaking of yourself in the third person. If I had a magic looking glass, I would have answered, "When he falls in love with The Wiggles," but I was pregnant and hadn't yet connected the dots to your love for Elmo and the way you were learning language.

In fact, Elmo saved us both through the early months of my pregnancy. You decided 5 a.m. wake up was the norm. No matter how much I extended cuddle and story time later into the evening, you would pop up ready to play at 5 a.m. every morning. Elmo let me lie down and try to get to 6 a.m. before beginning the play-with-me-mommy hours of our day. Toddlers are like little drunk adults— demanding and unreasonable at every turn of the day. So, after failed attempts to have you cuddle next to me, I'd waddle to the living room, stick in the DVD, and breathe a sigh of relief before nestling back under the covers in hopes of one more hour of rest.

I'd like to say I easily transitioned into the acceptance of television as a part of our lives, but I was still in the early phase of thinking I was in control of things. I still considered the television as a babysitter, a thing that needed to be limited. It surely was a mind-numbing distraction from the beauty of life.

This far out from the intensity of parenting young children, I can see and understand the one who was looking to be numbed out by the television was me. It was the only way I knew how to use a television as a result of the role it had played in my life. You, however, my sweet children, rarely sat still with your hand in a bag of potato chips while the program transported you out of your unhappy thoughts. You were dancing to the music, shouting out the answer, transforming yourselves into one of the characters and often gathering random items from around the house to mimic what you were seeing. You saw the platform in front of you the same way you saw the entire world around you—as a tool for learning. It was when I began to lay down my heartache that I was able to see through your fresh eyes and engage in TV with the same wonder you did.

This magical box could be turned on to find your friends waiting to go on an adventure with you or show you something you had never before seen and might not actually be able to see. It especially made you smile when you were perhaps feeling left out. And yes, from time to time it was used to distract you from the real heartbreak that is being a human who is moving through the complicated parts of being alive. It's stunning how often I, as a parent, expected you to be able to handle it all far better than I could.

There is a long list of television shows and characters that warm my heart at the mere mention of their names, as I immediately pull up memories of the younger version of the two of you fully immersed in the worlds created for you. I could also write a short novel about all the ways you took those shows and movies off the screen and into your very real lives to play with the characters and concepts until every nugget of learning was transformed into your understanding of the world.

Pass the remote,
Mama

ALL-ACCESS ONLINE PASS

Hello My Loves,

The internet was not around when I was growing up. In fact, it seemed to grow up alongside the two of you. The thing about new technology is that it is hard to parent around something that hasn't been around that long. Helping the two of you explore and stay safe around these new shiny technologies was some serious on-the-job training. I know there is a lot of information out in the world that talks about protecting children from things that could harm them by not giving them access to scary things. This collided with our approach to parenting, which was rooted in trust and honesty.

When the two of you became interested in video games at the ages of three and five, my instant thought was, *Not in my house.* Sure, go ahead and play those evil games at your friends' houses, but you will not bring them into our house. I know, the two of you, my rockstar gamers, are laughing as you read this. It wasn't an easy journey for me, but it was rooted in knowing that the relationship I wanted to have with the two of you was more important than any technology that tried to come between us.

When you, my firstborn, fell in love with hockey, *NHL 07* was hot on the market. I watched you use the game as a tool to broaden your understanding of the sport—how to play, how a team is built, the rules of the game, what broadcasting is, and so much more. In all honesty, it was the first time I started to look at video games as a learning tool and not a mindless activity. With this shift, we slowly brought more and more games into the house, and I witnessed your pure joy. Yes, of course, there were remotes thrown across the room when the games got too hard. There were countless arguments over whose turn it was. And there was a constant negotiation in my own mind as to what was too much. Yet, each time I took a breath and connected to what was happening in real-time, I saw the value even in the arguments and the meltdowns.

You were both pushing your edges and growing from there. You were trying something over and over and over again until you could improve your skill set to change the outcome. You were negotiating, problem-solving, and thinking way outside of the box to come up with creative solutions. Each time I was ready to pack away all the games and declare our home a tech-free zone, one of you would knock me on my butt with a skill or piece of knowledge only the game could have taught you.

Then along came the online world, where you could connect with your peers and others interested in gaming. I had to take the deepest breaths as I released you into an invisible world that was said to be full of dangerous humans looking to lure young children into trouble. I knew that limiting you would only make the internet a forbidden thing that you might try to access in secrecy, behind closed doors, and in ways that I wouldn't know about. So, we decided to give you an all-access online pass, welcoming this tool into our home, and keeping the doors wide open for honest conversations to happen.

You, my firstborn, were ripped off during an in-game exchange when you first started playing with other gamers. You had worked for days to build up your game currency so you could purchase a rare card. Then some devious human came along and promised to duplicate it for you, give you the card you wanted, then return your original rare card to you. This sounded perfect, so you agreed and transferred the card. But the guy disappeared, taking your card and giving you absolutely nothing. You were devastated. In your heartbreak, you turned to Dad and me. This is where we had the biggest chance as parents to impact your future online. The first thing we did was get upset with you. Then we listened to the story, the anguish, and the anger. We did not shame or blame you. We did not tell you what you should have done. We did not revoke any of your online access. We listened with open hearts while you worked through your feelings. Then we talked about how we could support you in regaining what you had lost. We helped you figure out how to report this person for his behavior. We had a brainstorming session on how to prevent such a thing from happening again. It was a respectful, collaborative process. From there, you were ready to handle anything that looked somewhat suspicious in future online encounters.

You, my second born, found yourself in a tricky situation on Skype when you first started using it alone. You were added to a call by a friend of a friend, and when the conversation went sideways, you left the call but didn't leave the group conversation. So, when I walked into your room the next morning, my mind did some serious freaking out when I saw words, names, and things way out of what is okay in our house. I knew what I did next was going to shape how you handled uncomfortable situations in the future. When you woke up, I asked about the conversation. You told me the entire story. I showed you how the conversation was still going on and that it made me uncomfortable. Turns out, you didn't know how to leave a conversation on Skype and found the noise of the messages coming in irritating, so you went to bed. I showed you how to leave a conversation on Skype. Then we chatted about adding folks you didn't know as friends and joining conversations with strangers. We talked openly about how to avoid strangers on the internet and what to do when they showed up without your consent. You decided you would come get me before adding a contact so we could decide together if it was a good idea, building from a young age a trust in your own ability to keep yourself safe in all environments.

All these years later, I know that had I used shaming, blaming, or punishment, I would have pushed the two of you away. The online world is here to stay. The best thing I could do was help you understand how to navigate through it, trust your intuition when things felt off, and support you unconditionally when you made mistakes. Recently, I asked you in total frustration, my second born, what you thought the difference was between you and the latest school shooter. I wanted to know because you had access to the same internet and video games that were being called out as part of the problem. I wanted to know, through your eyes, what made the difference.

You said, "The internet is a scary place, and without someone who loves you paying attention, you can get into a lot of trouble." In that one sentence, you so clearly stated that it was the love and attention that made the difference. So, it isn't about keeping harm away from children; it's about loving children to fill them all the way up, so they are not looking for attention somewhere else.

Yours in high-speed explorations,

Mama

LEAVING HOME AND CHASING DREAMS

Hello My Loves,

It was December of 2009. I don't remember the exact date, but we were nearing the holiday season, which, as you know, is much shorter in Canada than in the US. So, I'll say it was close to December 20th.

Dad walked in the back door, brow furrowed, stating, "You'll never believe what just happened."

Pushing the broom across the mud accumulating around the back door frame, I paused to listen.

"Mikey just asked if I wanted him to give my details to his boss at Apple. He thinks I would be a good fit for a position they are looking to fill."

You might not remember, but at the time, our garage was stacked high with every Apple box Dad had ever had his hands on. One box even contained his first iPhone, which had to be jailbroken (a term I never fully understood) to be used in Canada. To say he was an Apple fan would be an understatement. Dad calmed his bursting enthusiasm by assuming there was no way this would lead to much.

The next call came after a long weekend of anticipation. The Apple employee asked, "Would you be interested in working for

Apple?" and Dad proclaimed he would happily sweep the floors if that's what it took.

You both know what an enthusiastic Dad can look and sound like. His wildest dream was hanging within reach, and the smile across his face was unlike anything I had seen.

It's worth noting the different ways we fell into the understanding of what this meant for us all. Dad took the first vacation I had known him to take since our honeymoon, relaxing into the new PS4 to battle through *Uncharted*, with you, my second born, turned away behind the recliner, to avoid seeing the graphic images but still participate in the story. Staying up late into the night, dad battled through mission after mission to finally complete the entire game.

You'll probably remember at this time in our living together, Dad was working uncountable hours at two jobs that allowed him to make the money required to give us what we needed to thrive as a family. There were late hours, everyday, without pause for much else than sleep and food. To see him kicked back with a controller in hand was surprising for us all. And that should have been an indicator of what was to come. He'd already mentally left the old job for the one he had yet to secure.

I, on the other hand, buried my head into the sand of disbelief. There was no way I could imagine giving up living close to family with the secluded ocean and endless forest out my front door. To keep my mind at ease, I took a book to the couch while you two played blissfully with the new collection of toys you had received on Christmas. It was one of the best Christmas holidays. In hindsight, I can see how it was the calm before the storm.

The interview was set for Jan 10th 2010. We made a vacation of it. The four of us were in sunny California, entertaining the ridiculous notion of living in the Bay Area. The Cupertino Inn seemed fancy, serving both breakfast and happy hour just blocks from the famous Infinite Loop that Dad drove us around before even checking into our home away from home.

I can now see how well the entire thing was set up to impress us. On our first full day there, we drove to visit the San Jose Shark Tank just to see what the cost would be to take you, my hockey-loving firstborn, to your first NHL game. Of course, there was a game the next evening, and the tickets were cheaper than we could reason ourselves out of. Dad bought the tickets while the three of us stood, hands cupped around our eyes, pushing against the glass to get a peek inside. A man, seeing us, approached the doors as we backed up, certain we'd broken a rule. He welcomed us by asking what we were up to. Enthusiasm spilled out as I tried to capture your passion for the game in a few short sentences. Opening the door wider, he asked if we'd like a tour.

I know you both remember the awe of being inside the HP Center. Touring the dark hallways, we found the locker room where all the gear was drying. Even all these years later, I can't find the words to spin a tale worthy of the excitement of standing next to the gear of Nabokov (the San Jose Sharks goalie at the time) and getting the chance to slip his helmet on your head. This was the stuff of dreams.

Slipping our way across the ice, we found the Zamboni, the penalty box, and the home and away team benches. He pitched us the history of the San Jose Sharks, hoping to convert us to fans, I am sure. It would take far more than that to change generations of Canuck fandom, but he certainly amped up our appreciation for a town where hockey was less loved and much more available to the true fans.

As if this was not enough of a wow-this-place-is-amazing experience, we took you two to Chuck E. Cheese for dinner. Never had your little eyes seen something as magical as a place where you were immediately rewarded for your gaming prowess with tiny tickets spitting out of a machine. The tickets could turn into tiny treasures, growing in size with each game won.

Dad spent hours upon hours the next day in back-to-back interviews that threatened his on-time return for the big game. We waited patiently over boxes of newly purchased Lego sets that simply had to be built without any sense of how one packs a newly constructed Lego set in their bag to take on a plane. There was no reasoning. You, my firstborn, needed to build your Lego the moment the set was in your hands. And it was only with the lure of the Cartoon Network while snuggled in bed that I convinced you to pause.

Exhausted and hungry, Dad pulled up in our complimentary Mercedes Benz, and we dashed through rain puddles to join him. You, my second born, and I were headed back to the bright light bell-ringing wonder of Chuck E. Cheese while Dad and you, firstborn, piled your laps with overpriced hot dogs and popcorn. We were already living a bigger life than we had just days earlier.

It was on our final day in California, buckled in and heading toward San Francisco, that I had a thought—a feeling—that I put into words I sometimes wish I would have kept inside.

"I could live here."

Less than an hour later, pulling off the 280 toward Candlestick Park, Dad's cell phone rang to announce that the job was on the table. Pulling over, he tried to capture the details while I entertained the two of you, hungry and still not in love with driving farther than twenty minutes.

Here's a poem I wrote, in one of my old notebooks, to capture what those moments felt like to me.

> *We parked across from the ferry building in San Francisco, squirming hungry boys leapt from their car seats as I stared shocked at the price to park for just one hour.*
>
> *He's on the phone again, a dizzying grin across his face, asking the questions he forgot when the original job offer came in. Flabbergasted and irritated at the future moments he has left us for, I snap about, grabbing a hand to cross the street.*

The indoor market doesn't have a single familiar food place. The boys are running, touching, exploring every hands-off item within reach. Spinning through the specialty shop, I grab what I hope to be familiar enough to stave off declarations of starvation for the drive back. Scanning ingredient labels for nuts and wheat, he stands out of the eyeshot of both boys, still smiling at something I can't see.

I shepherd us all toward the check out to pay the price of a gourmet meal for a small collection of picnic snacks. We are out the door just in time for the sky to open up on us. It's the rainiest season the Bay Area has seen in decades.

Crossing back toward the car, the boys bolt for the grass-lined cement stacks, inviting climbing, jumping, energy releasing, and an urban playground. All I can see is trash, homeless humans, and harm not present in our small city life.

He's still lost in numbers, bonuses, and an excited reality that my ears cannot hear over the sound of imagined dangers the boys are stepping toward, dangling overpriced cheese in front of cold, wet, hungry humans.

Everything hinges on my willingness to leave behind everything I know in pursuit of a dream I just learned he had.

We, the three of us, were looking into the eyes of a man whose wildest dream was hanging just within reach. It felt impossible to offer anything other than a **"yes."** Less than a year earlier, we had written a family mission statement saying that we would always unite in our commitment to love one another unconditionally, and now we were being asked to walk the talk.

Wisely, Dad did not ask for an all-in "yes" at that point, he simply asked me, the more cautious one, to take the next step in the process. Quite honestly, when it comes to making life-altering transitions toward big, huge changes, all you really can do is say "yes" to the next logical step. Otherwise, you'll go tumbling into all the reasons why something is simply impossible, wrapping fear so tightly around the vision that the courage required to fully live is suffocated.

So, we agreed there on a San Francisco street corner to take the next step in viewing the contract and understanding what was being offered to us to see if it was enough. We agreed to make the next step that, as you know, would eventually lead to us four Vancouver Islanders landing in the middle of Silicon Valley without a single soul other than ourselves to rely on.

In case you ever forget, my dear sons, you can do the hardest of things with a sense of wonder, seeking the one next thing.

Forever in awe,

Mama

EXAMINING THE FLAWS OF "DO AS I SAY"

Hello My Loves,

There is this idea that is quite common in parenting where there is an expectation for children to do better than the parents who are raising them. It might be caught up in the idea that our offspring need to be better versions of who we are, and that if we just "train" you up right, we can bypass all the messy parts of ourselves.

I first noticed this quite clearly when the two of you were young. A friend of mine sent her "troubled" teen to stay with us for the weekend. The two of them were trying to work out their differences over the phone. She had yelled and hung up the phone. When she called me back to debrief, she said the words, "All he does is yell at me." I listened to her first, and when it was time to respond, I pointed out that she also only yelled at him. I then, in the gentlest way I could muster, asked where she thought he would have seen a model for a different response to conflict? This question helped her reframe her approach at that moment, but I think the lesson was bigger for me because I was so new to parenting.

You see, so often when your emotions got big or the two of you disagreed, I would rush into the room with my big, loud voice, and request you get along with a level of patience I most definitely was not demonstrating. This is one of those lessons I was going to find myself learning over and over and over again. It took checking in, outside of the big emotions, to ask myself, "Am I requiring my children to do better than I am doing at this moment?" I asked if my expectations of you were true to your ages and skill sets.

You, my firstborn, have worn clothes two sizes above what was expected at your age for most of your life. You surprised many people when they discovered your age and recognized their expectations of you had been way off. Even as your mom, who was there at your birth, I was guilty more than once of having expectations of you beyond your age and stage in the world. It is possible, as humans learning in the world, to appear to have something figured out when it is just your first or second time trying it. It is also true that, when your brother was born, I started having all kinds of wild expectations of you based on you being a "big brother" that now, when I look back at how little you were when he was born, I am shocked by.

I want you both to know, should you walk down the road of parenting, you sadly will have little to no control over how your child logs in their memory the experiences you have together. All you really can be responsible for is how you show up for that child, which will almost always be more about you doing the work you need to do than it will be about the child having to change to meet any expectations you carry around. It's a terribly bitter pill to swallow at times, especially in a world that, at the time of writing, will often blame a parent for a child's behavior instead of seeking out just what the parent might be doing to get in the way of meeting the child's needs.

Most children who are seen as misbehaving are actually trying to communicate an unmet need. Children are not out to disrupt their parents' lives; they truly are working to get their own needs met the best they can.

Yours in reality,

Mama

REALIZING I CAN'T BE
EVERYTHING YOU NEED

Hello My Loves,

I was not raised in a community, so when you came along, I think
I was under the impression that it would be up to me to do all the
things it took to raise you. My idealism had me wanting to be your
everything. I hoped I would be your go-to, your best friend, your
shining example of how to be an awesome human being.

Because I had not seen others welcomed into the sphere of
influence growing up, I thought raising you differently just meant
being a better version of myself, micromanaging every moment and
situation to influence the best possible outcome, and being on top
of every last bit of every last thing. Damn, I am tired from writing
this, let alone trying to live it.

The first time I started to get an inkling of the power of community was the summer of 2008 when we went to a camp out on
Salt Spring Island. I think the two of you remember it as the place
you started to fall in love with your dearest childhood friends. The
idea was that a group of like-minded families all gathered for a collection of days to simply be in community together. On the outside,
it looked like making crafts, playing music, dancing, and dining

each evening together. There was a pool, a lake, and three full days of time to play until I carried your tired bodies up to the tent where you would, without hesitation, dip into a deep, restful sleep.

What I started to see there was that the load I had placed upon my shoulders did not need to be carried alone. There were other families wanting to show up as fully for their children; we could do it together by intentionally creating space to gather, connect, and catch our breaths. These other humans became a part of your trusted team. They watched out for you with close to as much investment in your success as I did.

We spent many weekends and sometimes week-long events deep within this community, growing, learning, and connecting with families that lived both near and far. These events in and of themselves shaped who you became as humans on a deeper level. It was about the relationships and connections that you were making with humans who were not me.

I started to see there were humans in this community who would be able to meet your needs that I would never be able to. It was not because of a lack of information, but it was because they personally, as who they were in the world, delivered information in a way that was more palatable to you.

One who stands out (and I will forever be grateful for) is the human, Renee, who provided you with all kinds of information by creating no-shame zones over and over again for you to openly ask questions, explore curiosities, and laugh out loud at all the uncomfortable parts of moving through uncomfortable topics. Renee was not only a friend, but she was also a human willing to stand up for every child and advocate for a safe place to discuss sex, intimacy, and everything that goes along with that. I released a huge sigh of relief knowing she was in the world, creating opportunities for you to learn and grow when you weren't all the way comfortable talking about these things with me. As you both know, she became a cherished second mom in your lives who, to this day, would do anything within her power to advocate for your well-being.

Then there were those who showed up with information about something I didn't have in my wheelhouse. People throughout the years used to commend me for being able to "teach" you all the things we were learning at home together. I constantly pushed back with the fact I was not the knower of all the things or the teacher of them; my job was to gather resources and seek out mentors. This was the job I took on from the get-go. And oh boy, did we run into some awesome humans who wove their influences deeply throughout our family time together.

There was a big piece of me that needed to let go of being your most trusted source or go-to for all things. I think I got caught up in a romanticized idea of what our relationship would look like if I was constantly putting it at the forefront of our lives together—that doing so would get me one of those Hallmark movie connections with you forever. The first time I heard you trusted an adult who was not me with a piece of information dear to your heart, I thought I would break. I launched into the sort of shame spiral that had me questioning every part of who I was as your mother, relentlessly searching for the moment when I had obviously failed you.

Thank goodness for the power of amazing women in my life. I was able to pull my head back into reality and recognize that it truly does take a village to raise a human being. This saying came to mean that I made sure your world was full of trusted humans you could turn to with your hearts. It could not be about me needing to earn, prove, or compete to get your attention. It had to be about you being surrounded by the resources you needed to survive. Of course, I could never be all of that, which is a very small way of thinking. If you are to live the happy, full lives I want for you, it is going to take a whole team of human beings.

Once I could settle into the knowledge, I started to see just how beautiful the community around us was. I became a fierce defender of whom we let in and who got to stay. I also began to trust you over and over and over again, my sweet sons, as you told me, based on your intuition, who was valuable and who was harmful. I apologize once again for those instances when I forced a connection to go on beyond what you declared to be enough. You have both always been keen observers of those humans who were there to build us up, and I, with my baggage, did not always have such a clear picture of what was going on.

I write this piece to you and encourage you to always surround yourself with the kind of community that wants to see you thrive, genuinely desires your best interests to be met, and is often asking, "how can I contribute to your well-being?" Also, look around at those who are in your life and ask yourself the same questions: "How can I contribute to their well-being? How can I improve upon my community?" The world might try to tell you that all the big changes happen far away or with grand gestures, but I am here to tell you to focus on the places where you actually have influence and grow there.

Yours in community,

Mama

LISTEN MORE, TALK LESS

Hello My Loves,

Before I met you, I think I had only ever understood how to listen to respond. I didn't know that there was any other kind of listening. You've both taught me over and over and over again that there is a sort of listening that is about the emptying of a heart. It does not require a response; in fact, responses can get in the way of this sort of witnessing. I think Thich Nhat Hanh describes it best when he defines compassionate (or deep) listening as the kind of listening that relieves the other person of their suffering. The only purpose you have as the listener is to create a container for the person to empty their heart into.

This is the listening the two of you have introduced me to. I admit, I am still working on it. It's one of those skills I imagine I will be working on for my entire lifetime. I still get confused and think that when you bring me your big-hearted observations, thoughts, or ideas, it is my role to finish the sentence for you and then hit the ground running with my troubleshooting skills. I can see now how that robs you of your agency and leaves you feeling rescued, not necessarily emptied out and leaning into your own skill sets.

There are times when advice-giving is needed. Knowing when it is, is not about mind reading; it is simply about asking, "Do you want my help, input, or suggestions?" It's as simple as asking you what you want instead of launching into proving to some invisible spectator my mad, out-of-the-box, Herculean problem-solving abilities.

When you were working your way out of diapers, my firstborn, I used all kinds of problem-solving to step in and make this happen for you. Okay, for me, I had two children, was up to my elbows in poopy diapers, and was absolutely certain that my need to change that could will you into some form of compliance. I tried to force a number of solutions on you (as you can read in the potty-training section of this book). You tried with all the skills of a three-year-old to tell me what you needed.

I see how I was listening to solve, not listening to hear what you were saying. You were not ready, but you would be in your own time. Might I add, when you did get there on your own, it was seamless.

I think adults get confused in parenting, thinking they need to have all the answers, information, or expertise when the art of it is learning to listen deeply to the human in front of them in a way that lets the human empty their own heart. When we meet each other, then we get to move forward side by side looking for ways to partner.

Yours in all kinds of messy mistakes,
Mama

AN UNCONVENTIONAL PATH

Hello My Loves,

I should have known the moment I decided to birth you at home that we were not heading down a conventional path. I've recently started to think of this a little bit differently and want to write you a letter of apology.

You see, I realized I wanted this unconventional path. Along the way, I believed with every part of who I was that it was the right thing for us. I even fell into the trap of thinking it was the right thing for everyone. I stood on stages and told parents how they should parent their children. My mind, trained through white supremacy, believed I knew how to parent every child—that people simply needed to follow my lead.

It was with great humility that I came to understand all I knew how to do was parent a couple of white boys, as a married, cisgendered, heterosexual woman, with financial security. It stopped me for quite some time from putting pen to paper to talk about the world of living alongside the two of you and what I was learning.

My other humbling moment arrived when talking to a friend whose son had determined she had harmed him by the parenting path she chose. In that conversation, I heard myself say, "This unconventional path is what we wanted for them, and it is true they may not have chosen it for themselves." It's rather gutting to recognize you've spent a lifetime working toward something that may be the thing that's the center of someone else's childhood regrets.

So, I am here now on this page to say to you, "I am sorry." I am sorry if this is not what you hoped your childhood would look like. I am sorry if you have launched out into the world without the skills you feel you need to track down success. I am sorry for making the sort of choices and decisions that may conflict with the ones you would have made for yourself if you were standing where I was standing.

I also invite you to bring it all to me. I will sit and listen with the same open heart that had me chasing down alternative ways to love you in a world that sees children as an inconvenience. I will love you with the same fierce love that had me tuck you next to me in bed when the experts claimed it would harm you. I will reflect on every word with the same commitment that found me pouring over literature about child development and personal strength.

I will, no matter your words, reflections, or takeaways, stand strong as the mother you need me to be as you become the adults you want to be.

Yours in reflection,
Mama

YOU ALWAYS HAVE A CHOICE

Hello My Loves,

I was having one of those meltdowns that I am well known for, where I was convinced that the entire fate of our family rested on my ability to keep the entire house clean. When I was growing up, what I knew was that the woman was the one who kept the house in order. Gram was still rooted in the generation that believed a woman's place was in the home. Even though I grew up knowing I wanted to do something different, that these were old ideas, I had a ton of internalized sexism working against me.

The first time I walked into your dad's home, there was a kitty litter box the size of a Rubbermaid container overflowing with waste from the cat weighed down under her matted hair. The kitchen was a home for dirty dishes and a petri dish of mold masquerading as a rice cooker. Cleaning wasn't high on his list of things to do in day-to-day living.

Before marriage, we talked about roles and the world around us, agreeing we both held the same value of equity and would share the load as a team going forward. Some things, though, are ingrained into our bones so deeply that we fall into them without even noticing. I was playing the role of a dutiful wife without ever taking it outside of my actions to see if they matched my value system.

Also, Dad got up each day and made money to provide for our family. I was lost under the construct of capitalism that deemed his worth, attached to dollars, much higher than my own. The result had me hustling to clean every surface without requesting assistance because that was how I could prove my worth.

Walking heavy footed around each corner and slamming into my own resentment, I was certain if I did not claim this important responsibility, we would all perish under the toxic buildup. You, my firstborn, looked me dead in the eyes and said, "You don't have to do any of it, mom. You know you have a choice."

I'd like to say I stopped dead in my tracks, wrapped my arms around your young self, and proclaimed deep gratitude for your wisdom. But instead, I fought back, desperate to hold on to my old ideas because, without them, who was I?

You, wise beyond your years, met me eye to eye and said, "Mom, no one is going to die if you don't clean up."

Ha. Outsmarted by an eight-year-old stating the obvious from a place of pure logic, not one of defiance. You were, without a doubt, one hundred percent correct. I had a choice not only in whether I cleaned the house, but also in how I cleaned the house. If I didn't want to do it, which based on the stomping and ranting was most likely true, I did not have to. If I was going to, mop in hand, huff and puff my way to a shiny floor, I might as well adjust my attitude if I refused to put the mop down. I was irritated that no one else had the same need for cleanliness as I did and was too damn stubborn to ask for help. The guidance of inward reflection that you demanded by holding tight to your truth of, "you have a choice, Mom," has guided me through more than one backwards tumble into the world of misplaced obligations.

Yours in cleanliness,
Mama

PLEASE, CAN WE NOT BE A JUDGY FAMILY

Hello My Loves,

I remember the first time I leaned over to Dad and dropped something that could only be defined as judgment toward a family member. You, my firstborn, looked me in the eyes and said, "Please, can we not be the kind of family that talks bad about each other?" I was stopped in my tracks. You see, I was used to this combination of gossip and sarcasm. For me, this was the norm, and in fact, I didn't have a ton of experience gaining favor without an exchange of gossip. I was also used to using sarcasm as a way to express displeasure and quickly withdraw my complaint if it offended the person receiving it by using the line, "I was just kidding." So, the moment when you honestly asked me to do better was rather profound.

You were asking clearly for what you wanted in the world from the relationships around you. I took it to mean that you wanted them to be kind, predictable, and steeped in unconditionality, which I had learned to give you from the moment I met you. In fact, I didn't want to give you anything but that. In this instance, however, you were asking me to give that to all the people you loved, and that was something I had not recognized in myself yet. It was a tough pill to swallow and even tougher was the ask to consider my ways of communicating in the world with everyone because you were watching, learning, and wanting more than what I had displayed up to this point.

I wish I could remember what I was saying the day you asked me to be a better version of myself so that I had a better story to tell. The details don't matter though, because the idea was there: *do better*. When I think back to my formative years, most of the time, the best way to get the attention I was looking for was to side with my parents on whatever was being said. There was a great use of blame and gossip as a protective measure. It's a by-product of growing up alongside alcoholism. When you asked me to do better, I really wasn't sure where to begin, so I started by literally biting my tongue when things that were negative or sarcastic sprang to my mind. The two of you will chuckle as you read this, as I am so not an expert at this even all these years later. I am still guilty of slipping into survival tactics when I am stressed, tired, or not being present with what is right in front of me.

I am forever grateful to both of you for asking me to do better, drop the judgment, and try to show up day in and day out as the best version of myself. It's true I likely fail at this as often as I succeed. I thank you for asking me to keep trying to find ways to reduce the harm I cause in the world.

Becoming better one mistake at a time,
Mama

TENDING A MIND IS A PRECIOUS THING

Hello My Loves,

I think it can be easy in this world to think all days have to be happy days. The truth is that some days are going to be hard; they are going to suck. You may even be in a place where you can look around and see everything you need to be happy and still feel unhappy. That is okay.

I am pretty sure by now you know that humans in our family have had some mental health challenges. When I was growing up, none of this was talked about. In fact, mental health struggles were seen as character flaws or someone's weakness. Mental health, like physical health, needs tending. And sometimes, cells grow together or experiences happen that make things mutate. It is no one's fault. We would never blame a person for having cancer, so why is it that we blame a person for being depressed?

You are both on your own journeys that will include ups, downs, and curves that may or may not lead you to need extra support. Please never hesitate to go and see a therapist or even take medicine if it is needed to bring you back into the life that you long to live.

There is never *ever* any shame in doing what is required for your unique self and body to find contentment in the world.

I grew up hearing stories of a nana who had two nervous break-downs. I never knew what that meant or looked like. There was no room for conversation. This same grandmother was my biggest fan. She thought the world of me. And even though I do not advocate for having favorites, I was hers. It was confusing to me to hear stories of her weakness that led to her ending up in what was then called the "loony bin." All I saw was a woman, living through great loss, who loved to talk to me about my growing legs and how they might stop me from attracting a boyfriend.

I remember becoming curious and wondering what a nervous breakdown looked like. As I grew up and started understanding the complexities of the world, I tried a few times to get more details. You know I didn't come from the sort of people who talked about the hard things out in the open. It was more of a drink-it-into-forgetting kind of style. So, I was met mostly with, "I don't know," and subject changes.

There came a time when I knew if I was going to be the mom the two of you needed me to be, there was some work I was going to need to do. The sort of work that meant pulling back the curtains and taking a good, long, hard look at what was holding me back from living my fullest life. This is when I started going to therapy. I had always been reading and growing in my well-being, but there are some things that require professional help. That's just the truth of it.

When I was first diagnosed with an anxiety disorder and PTSD, I was filled with shame. When I was in my young adulthood, I blamed Gram for her anxiety. I was certain I would never be some-one who had anxiety attacks; I would somehow battle my way through all the hard parts and come out stronger. I think I believed I could "positively think" my way out of my mental health strug-gles—that I could or should be able to simply use willpower to heal my injured places all by myself. This simply was not true.

Now I am not negating the powers of these tools at all. In fact, I use a number of tools I learned pre-therapy to keep myself grounded and in check a good majority of the time. I journaled, meditated, and exercised, but I still needed a therapist to help me see my blind spots and work my way to the other side of them. I needed someone who could look me in the eye, without any history or emotions, and challenge what I was saying as absolute truth.

I know the two of you have heard stories, and I've shared about what it was like for me growing up—the places where trauma touched and informed the human I am now. Through the support of therapy, I learned that I was shaped by those experiences, but they were not who I was in the current moment. Inside of my own head, I could get trapped in a place where it seemed as though I was broken or responsible or forever doomed to repeat the ingrained patterns. I'll never forget the moment one of my therapists looked at me and asked the basic question, "What if that wasn't true?" At first, I tried to argue my way out of the situation to prove I knew what I was talking about. She looked at me and said, "What if it was no longer true?" You see, sometimes I can believe so much that something is right or true that I simply can't let go of it. She posed questions and offered me ways to free myself from that which was holding me back, while also helping me create my own stories and ways forward to see the truth that settled into the moment I was living in instead of pulling me backward toward something no longer in existence.

Support groups comprised of people with similar challenges are another beautiful avenue to gather healing. The first time I stepped into an Adult Children of Alcoholics meeting, I wept. I cried for the full hour-long meeting and had so much choked in my throat that I could not engage with the kind people offering further support at the meeting's end. I dashed out the door, sat in the car, and wept out the hurts I thought were mine to carry alone for all of my tomorrows. Here was this room for all strangers carrying the same weight and offering a way to put it all down.

We've talked throughout the years about the generational alcoholism that exists in our family. I want the disease out in the open so we can heal our way forward. Just because I am not an alcoholic does not mean you were saved from the side effects of alcoholism. It's been a long journey, and I know I didn't name it early enough to protect you from my behaviors that tied into it all. Please know I will always be open to hearing these harms and how they have shaped you in the world. I will always support whatever ways you do or do not engage in finding the meaning of this in your being.

I hope you will always place deep kindness and generosity around your mental health and value it the same way you do your physical well-being.

Humbly yours,
Mama

IT'S AN UNJUST WORLD

Hello My Loves,

We live in an unjust world. I know this is likely something you already know through my rants and frustrations as we've gone about living together. I am putting it down here so that you never forget its truth. I hope before I leave this planet that I will have to come back and tear this page out of the book because it no longer holds true, but at this moment, I don't believe that will occur. I will die trying to change it, though.

My wildest dream is that any child you choose to bring into this world will never know injustice. You two stand at the top of the pillar of privilege, with your white, male, and cisgendered, heterosexual ways. You have a power most don't: to demand change. I am bold enough to say it is your responsibility to do so. Until those with the most power say, "Enough is enough. We will not carry on this way," nothing will change to the degree necessary to reach true justice.

When I was growing up, the injustice I felt in my bones was for children, and that is likely what took me on the path to being the mother that I have been to you. I could never understand how people could be mean to a child simply because they were smaller and less experienced in the world. I never understood the need or necessity for children to fit into an adult world. It all seemed like an unfair advantage stacked on the side of those who had more power.

I remember when I was starting my career as a teacher. There were schools in the district that had fewer resources than other schools. They were the communities where parents had less money and resources available to them. I remember asking why we weren't giving those schools more supplies than the schools in the higher-income areas that had stay-at-home parents and resources to spare. I was taught quickly that is not how our world works. If you have money, you get more. And that's not just in what you can afford to pay for but in the quality of free education you have access to, the homes you can live in, and the foods available in the buildings around you.

The world right now believes that this sort of thing is something you can work your way out of, and that simply is a lie. It's told by those with more so they don't have to feel bad about overspending on luxuries while those just a few miles away can't afford to feed their children. It's a direct product of capitalism.

I am as guilty of this as those I point my judgmental fingers at, so I will continue to spend my days examining and calling out the places where I can do better at living by my principles. It's easy in theory to talk about losing something so someone else can have more, but we've been trained by a system that puts ourselves at the center and places others as an idea outside of us. The truth is, we also are harmed by the system of injustice because a part of us must cease to feel in order to tolerate a world that is so tipped out of a balance that human decency is on the ballot every single time voters go to the polls.

Even as I sit here claiming I will keep fighting for a just world to give future generations, I am also untangling the parts of me that cling to my comfort time and time again—the moments when I choose a path of least resistance and negotiate in the space of my mind that I am somehow deserving. I know, deep down, that for me to have more, there is someone else who has less.

All of this is to say to you, my dear children, I hope your hearts will always remain open enough that you question your every move and more times than not choose to use what you have to contribute to making the world a safer, more just place for all. I know from living with you that you both have the capacity to love beyond what is comfortable, and I hope you will use this as your moral compass always.

In hope and discomfort,
Mama

KNOWING YOU AND HEALING ME

Hello My Loves,

It was not until the day that I met each of you that I knew how deeply I needed to be healed. I had made it through university with an honors degree, lived overseas, traveled to faraway places, and fallen in and out of love, all the while thinking I was a full human being. Then you arrived, and the moment your eyes looked into mine, all my broken pieces tumbled onto the floor between us. It was no longer good enough to just get by coping with numbing distractions. I had to be more than I had ever been because you handed me, in that brief moment, my first experience of true, unconditional love.

I could not have named it at the moment, though. I thought perhaps it was something that people called the mama bear feeling—this deep desire to protect you from a world that seemed to be snared with traps at every turn. It was accompanied by the absolute knowing that a loss of you would be perhaps the only thing in this lifetime that I could not actually survive.

I don't think our world encourages people to look at themselves and wonder if they have what it takes to care for a child. There is an unspoken way, or at least there was in my upbringing, that we are meant to grow up, fall in love, and produce children. To the extent that the first time I met a woman who had decided not to have children, I was stunned. I sat back and wondered, *Had I ever decided to have children?* I mean, of course, I had talked to Dad about having children and when we would and if we were ready. But I don't think this was ever made from a place of understanding that I had a choice to not use my reproductive organs. It sounds funny, I know, because with every fiber of my being I have been a mother for the last nineteen years. I just wanted it noted here, in these letters to you, that it is not necessary to have children; they require a great deal of you, so it's okay to want your life to be about something different.

Now back to my breaking apart. You see, the two of you required me to be more than I had been previously. In order to do that, I had to do a lot of self-discovery—pull my insides out, turn them outside, lay them out, and have a good hard look at what was working and what simply needed to be adjusted. I wish I could tell you a tale of how eloquently I did all of this with intention, commitment, and all kinds of winning, but that's just not the truth of any of it. It mostly looked like me making the same mistakes over and over and over again until one of you turned to me with big words or actions and demanded a different response. Stuck in the loop of repeating my mistakes, I would put pen to paper, pour it out and find my way to a deeper place of understanding. It wasn't just about understanding you, but it was also about understanding me—the place where I needed some love.

You, my firstborn, were my guinea pig. I was certain if I did the same thing day after day at the same time, we would be rocking this new relationship in no time. Here's the thing, you probably already know you aren't much for routines. You are more of a go-with-the-flow-of-the-day kind of human. This has been true since the beginning, not for lack of trying on your mother's part. It almost seemed, back in those early days, that the harder I tried to get you to fit into the routine, the more you resisted to the point that I was on the phone weeping, trying to find someone who could show me how to get you into a routine. Okay, truthfully, I wanted to know how to get you into my routine. Thank goodness for the sweet woman I stumbled upon who told me to get into bed with you and just rest together. That my worry was likely causing all the fuss that was happening between the two of us. She was right. My chill allowed me to find your rhythm. It wasn't attached to a clock or a to-do list; it was simply there in the moments between us where I could "hear" just what it was you needed.

You, my second born, had to conform to your older brother. As much as I would like to write you a sweet story about listening to what you had to teach me in those first few months, honestly, it was about fitting you into your big brother's life. He had words, tantrums, and legs that could run on his side. You were super portable, so I would say you found your rhythm within the chaos that was living life with a toddler. This taught me so much about the many positions a baby can sleep and nurse. You were by birth order simply more flexible in the early years. We, as your family, may have taken advantage of that for a little too long. I remember the day you finally put your foot down and refused to be convinced into what we wanted you to do. You see, prior to this point, if the three of us agreed on something, we could almost always convince you into thinking it was a great idea too. But not this day. You found your voice, and you were not going to be eating at what we had decided was the best choice of restaurants. I remember how hard your dad and brother continued to pressure you in the same moment when I began to really hear you, there in all your confidence, demanding to have an equal voice. Much to their frustration, I stepped in and agreed to side with you. All future family negotiations became more challenging for sure, but they also became far fairer and more inclusive of all family members.

This was the beginning of how the two of you launched me on my own healing journey. I hope the last example touches a bit of the edges of me that had to melt away in order to expand into what you needed of me as your mother. I am, after all, the one who invited you to this party. And as much as the world tried to tell me it was your job to fit in, I knew from a place deep inside of me that it was my job to heal so you could thrive.

Yours in healing,
Mama

I'M A RECOVERING PERFECTIONIST

Hello My Loves,

Here is something you may or may not know about me: I am a recovering perfectionist. I did not know this about myself until I was sitting in a therapist's office getting support for postpartum depression. She gently suggested some of my paralysis and over-whelmingness might be tied to perfectionism. I stopped and sat with that for the briefest of moments before rejecting the idea. I was certain that I had never done a single thing perfectly in my life. She went on to explain that it was perfectionism that stopped me from trying just about anything—certain I could not live up to my self-imposed standards. She also suggested it was what was driving me to attempt to get everything absolutely right with you, my then infant firstborn son.

You see, when I met you, all I wanted to do was make sure every single thing you experienced was rose-colored awesomeness. Each time your body let out a cry, I wanted to be there with the exact solution you needed. I was on mega high alert. You likely know that it is impossible to do this. Babies don't have words and often cry for reasons that are outside of what makes sense to the mind of their caregiver. I tied all your tears to my failings, weeping myself to sleep each night, I was certain I had already failed you. The therapist directed me to resources that would support me in putting down the burdens of perfectionism and leaning instead into the art of being fully human.

I wish I could write here that it was her who freed me of my attachment to perfectionism and that the little beast never came back to haunt me. But you would see right through those lies since you have been living with me all these years and watching me slay the dragon every single time it rears its head. It is a part of my recovery as an adult child of alcoholism to continually rewrite the parts of me that used these survival skills to make it through some of the hard parts of growing up.

The negative outcome of my perfectionism often looked like one of two things: surrendering or losing my cool. I suspect that your memories are most likely tied to the moments when I lost my cool. The surrender almost always happened under the covers once you had gone to bed and was replaced with a new zest to love you fiercely by the time our eyes met the next morning. Losing my cool, though, was loud. The example that comes to mind right now, my sons, was the day on the lake when I was rowing us into the wind. With sweat and frustration pouring down my face, you, my oldest, gently said, "You can do it, Mom," and I turned to you with the rage of an injured animal and shouted, "Don't encourage me." We've laughed at the story throughout the years. It was a moment of less than perfection when all the things fell apart for me, and I lashed out. The thing I did learn early enough on my journey as your mother, which I think saved me from my own perfectionism, was the art of apologizing.

Every single one of us is going to lose our cool time and time again in this world of being human. It is just a part of cycling through stress, heartbreak, and all kinds of hard things. We can learn the art of apologizing. Apologizing does not erase the harm that was caused by a misstep, but it does name it and lays the groundwork for forgiveness. It does not guarantee forgiveness; it opens the door to the potential for it. Owning of your wrong is one part of apologizing; the second is naming the harm you have caused. The part for me that was often the hardest was the required listening. It was never enough for me to walk in, drop a "sorry" next to an excuse, and leave the room. I had to name my error and then listen to your feedback. Sometimes it was a quiet, "It's okay mom," where I could still see the residue of my explosion in the corners of your eyes. Often, my only offer was, "I will try to do better next time." I had to fight the urge to promise I would never again do the thing I was apologizing for because life has shown me that is not a realistic thing to offer up. I was destined to make messier mistakes and was not going to overpromise and underdeliver on this one.

I do think, through the years and my countless apologies, I was showing you something. Perhaps I was showing you how to apologize for yourself, or maybe it was just creating a stage for you to make your own big, messy mistakes. Either way, I think the art of apologizing was the only thing that made it possible for me to continue working my way out of the trap of perfectionism that longed to rob me of the ability to be there for all the parts of your and my growth..

Yours in true Canadian sorry fashion,
Mama

YOU ARE ENOUGH

Hello My Loves,

I have to make sure that you understand something extremely important. You have inherited some things that do not belong to you. There was a moment in your existence when you, Gram, and I existed inside of the same body. That means, whatever was whirling around in her world left a mark on your DNA. If you want to read more about the science behind this, I recommend you read the book, *It Didn't Start with You: How Inherited Family Trauma Shapes Who We Are and How to End the Cycle,* by Mark Wolynn. I think it is important to understand this because there will be times when you have a response to the world that might not make sense based on your lived experience and that will maybe confuse you. When I am able to remember the relatives who came before me, I can sort out if what is troubling me is my lived experience or not. There was a time, my second born, when you were dealing with a fear that I was having an affair. You knew in your rational mind that it was not happening, yet still, when I would leave to go to the chiropractor, your body would have this reaction that left you thinking I was off to ruin my marriage. At first, I could not find a place in our family history that could explain this to you—a way that your DNA had been imprinted with a story of abandonment. Then one year, Gram sent me some family history documents and within that was a letter from your great-great grandmother's first husband. They had journeyed together from England to Canada, and once settled, your great-great grandmother had fallen in love with a visiting friend. The two left, leaving behind your great-great grandmother's husband and two daughters. She went on to marry this second man and have the family that ultimately led to both of our existences. Still, this story might explain where your fear of my falling in love outside of my marriage may have come from. The story itself fascinates me, and I was especially shocked that I had not heard it before reading this letter.

I am writing to you both about this because I think it is important to know that sometimes we will have reactions to the world that are not about what we are living through but about what those before us lived through. Even though neither Dad nor I are alcoholics, you both have been impacted by the generations of alcoholism that came before you simply because I was impacted from growing up with it in my home. I was way into my 30s before I realized that this had an imprint on my own experience of the world and that it was not something I could just push my way through. They have a name for that called "white knuckling," and it's not a way to handle true healing. It's basically holding on tightly and hoping you can make it through to the other side. I learned through therapy and support groups that the only true way to handle it all is to name it, look at it, and develop new tools of support in moving forward in the reality that is the life before me.

I know, by living with me, you have seen some of that growth throughout the years. You are also likely aware of many of the tools I have used to support myself through this. I will, as a reminder for you two, jot down a couple of my favorites. Always move your body. As my high school gym teacher would say to us, "When life gets hard, get out there and get your happy hormones hopping." This has supported me both in the movement piece of the endorphins and the being outside part. Over the years, both of you, have been able to enter the moment more clearly by stepping out into the fresh air. It's like whatever energy is holding you back has more room to move. I also think that fresh air has magic laced in its molecules that pull us way more clearly into the now moments. Secondly, there is meditation. I don't mean the sort that has you sitting still on a pillow for hours on end trying to empty your busy mind. I am talking about natural meditation that is tied to breathing deeply into your knowing and truth. Author Dean Sluyter writes about natural meditation in a totally accessible and relatable way if you need some guidance on this.

Lastly on this topic, I hope you can be ever so gracious with yourselves at every step of your life. Tune in to your individual definition of success and walk from that place. The world needs what you uniquely have to offer, but that may not look like what anyone else is up to because it is hardwired in you. The world of capitalism that you were born into operates only if you are left feeling like you need to hustle for your worth. As your mama, I am here to tell you that you do not have to. You do not have to define your success outside of yourself. You are now, and always have been, enough. Move from that place and you will always be making the world a better place.

With grace,
Mama

AUTHORITY OVER YOUR BODY

Hello My Loves,

Before meeting the two of you, I don't think I had ever heard the word "consent." Or maybe I had heard the word, but I certainly was not raised with the understanding that I had any sort of authority over my body. From teachers telling me when to pee and move my body, to parents controlling the what and when of my eating, to other humans taking advantage of my body, it took me a long time to realize I could say, "No."

I don't think I realized in the early years that the way I was living alongside you was teaching you about consent far before it had anything to do with sex. From the moment we started on-demand feeding, basically nursing whenever your bodies asked for it, we started what would continue to give you authority over your bodies.

There are many letters throughout this book that share with you moments when I let go of the sounds of the outside world and instead listened to what it was you knew about your own body. I wanted to make sure, there was an entire letter pointed to giving you a path toward consent. Honestly, I didn't realize that was what I was doing at the time, and I want to make sure you start out knowing all of that should you ever choose to become a parent.

The way we help humans understand consent when they are super-duper young is by letting them decide who can touch their bodies. It sounds all kinds of simple when I write it out like that, but in a world where adults seem to think they have power over children, it's not as easy as those words make it sound. It means letting a baby's body language let you know if they are comfortable being held, potentially offending grandparents by not forcing a child to hug or kiss them, or asking well-meaning uncles to only tickle a child after they've asked for permission first. The armor you will need involves remembering that what you are giving your child is far more powerful than the insults that may be tossed your way. I was poked fun at, talked about, and ridiculed, but when it came time to talk to the two of you about consent, you looked at me like I had three eyeballs. Never had it come into your minds that it was okay to force what you wanted on to another human, especially not physically.

If we want to change a world that blames a woman for what she is wearing when she is raped, it starts by making it the norm for children to set and hold their own boundaries around personal space. The tricky way this comes into play is when we control food and hygiene as well. I know this is tricky for so many parents confused by the ideas of health and wellness. I promise you, my sons, if you let your children listen to their own bodies around nourishment, they will develop a healthy-for-them relationship with it. Take the two of you, for example, you have had access to all the foods you wanted and can now list what makes you feel good and what makes you feel yucky. I, however, have spent decades trying to undo the harm of diet culture and the internal war between me and food. In fact, as I write this book, I am finally coming to understand that food is not a reward or a comfort; it is a tool of nourishment. I am understanding what it means to fuel my body to reach the goals of health that I have created for myself.

Hygiene is another super tricky one for most parents. I think it's easy to get caught up in thinking that our children are a representation of our worth or success in the world. This world somehow equates a "clean" child with a "good" parent, so it can be a challenge to let your child walk around with the side effects of the messy magic that is playing. I know we struggled to let you, my firstborn, walk into church in Spiderman pj's, or stand at the head of the table completely nude, but it was essential for you to build a sense of self in the world. I think people undervalue a child's ability to understand etiquette. When you have the freedom to wear what you want and clean up when it feels right, then you can willingly put on your shoes when your parent asks you to because it is something the store needs. When rules are arbitrary based on parents' ideas, the child becomes less willing to put on shoes because it all feels like being told what to do because "I said so." It was also my experience that, because we had a foundation of trust, when I encouraged you to shower because you weren't smelling so great, you trusted me and hopped in the shower. Neither one of you was interested in offending people with your smell. It's again an example of how partnering with a child instead of lording power over them can lead to a path toward everyone getting what they need.

I share all these pieces of consent so you can see the importance of starting far before anyone is considering an intimate relationship with a partner. It is laying a foundation of consent that leads to an understanding that individuals have authority over their bodies, and as such, there is no room for any misunderstandings when it comes time to engage in intimate relationships.

Yours in consent,

Mama

LOSING GRANDPARENTS

Hello My Loves,

I have watched the two of you lose both of your grandfathers. You've read about the first one and how it broke me open to the idea that I would never possibly be able to bubble wrap the world for you. The second time, I learned just how capable the two of you were of doing hard things and having compassion.

"Gump," as we called him, left his physical body in January of 2015. The two of you had spent more time with him on a computer screen than in real life. The few visits you had were confusing because he was being pulled away by his illness. But your hearts knew him well and loved him just the same.

Within twenty-four hours of his death, we were on an airplane headed across the country and into another to show up for our family. You never once complained about early morning plane rides or the disruption of your current schedules; you wrapped your arms around your sobbing father and said, "Let's go."

We were living in California then, so if the temperatures dropped below zero, it was only once a year for an hour or two during the night. In Brockville, Ontario however, the temperature dips deep below zero for months on end. So, we showed up with our California wardrobes, layered the best we could to endure -15°C temperatures.

You, my firstborn, initially dressed yourself in one of your grandfather's suit jackets and a pair of his shoes, while I conquered my fear of driving in winter conditions to buy, return, and rebuy the pants that would tie your outfit all together.

At this point in our lives, I had been criticized more than once for being the sort of parent that was willing to go out of the way to make your worlds as joyful as I could. Comments about you needing to experience hardship or that I was spoiling you made the rounds from time to time, and I listened with a tiny bit of worry growing in my mind. It's hard to walk a path you are carving on your own outside of what families around you are doing.

Each time I found myself at the edge, that place where I wondered if I should enforce my will upon the two of you, I'd find a spark in your eyes. It was the one that remained lit, curious, and well-loved, and I'd remember my original commitment to love you right where you were, not where I thought you should be.

I think adults have this idea that children need to practice doing hard things in order to be able to do them well. The theory was that I was robbing you of this skill by not making you suffer. Yet, you were required to stand at the door of a funeral home in a receiving line for four hours, two days in a row, and shake hands with strangers who were there to pay their condolences, and you did it without a single complaint. You showed up for your heartbroken Dad the same way he showed up for you every single time your hearts broke. This is what I want the world to know. Parents do not need to impose hardship on a child to prepare them for handling it. All that is required is that kind of love that turns children toward knowing they can do hard things.

When you meet children's needs alongside them and love them there, they learn, see, and gain experience in doing the same. If you ignore, punish, or inflict your own agenda on children, that is what they will know how to do.

Every time that you both have had to get all kinds of uncomfortable for the people you love, you have chosen to do so. You could have hidden in the downstairs rooms of the funeral home on the devices you brought along, but you never once did. You stood tall beside your cousin, your Dad, and me and answered all the ridiculous questions about schools you didn't even go to.

In gratitude,
Mama

CHOOSING TO DO BETTER

Hello My Loves,

I was three or four years old when I received my one and only spanking. The conversation went like this:

Gramps: "Shannon, did you put your clothes in the laundry basket?"

Me: "Yes".

Gramps: "Are you sure?"

Me: "Yes."

Gramps: "You put them all the way into the laundry basket?"

Me: "Yes."

Gramps: "I am going to ask you one more time. Did you put your clothes in the laundry basket?"

I am not sure if I was too far in, overcommitted to the lie, or oblivious to the fact that Gramps clearly knew I had not put my clothes in the laundry basket, but I still answered in the affirmative.

Gramps walked me to the door of the laundry room, where it was clear that I had only thrown my clothes toward the basket. He looked at me and said, "I thought you said you put your clothes in the laundry basket," to which I replied, "Lisa must have thrown them out." I was super committed to my story at this point.

He took me over his knee and gave me a spanking. I was appalled and scurried to the top bunk of my bed, pulling my knees as tight to my body as I could. Sometime later, Gramps climbed up the ladder while I pulled myself tighter inward and told me, "Shannon, that hurt me more than it hurt you."

I did not believe him for one second. There was a trust that had been broken, and there was no way his rear end was as sore as mine at that moment. Up until that day, I had followed my Dad around and been absolutely smitten with him. The lore is that my first sentence was, "Doin' Dad?" as I wandered around behind him. I was the perfect daddy's little girl. He was true to his learning at that moment, though, and never laid a hand on any of us after that.

I wish we had more years together so I could have asked him more about what it was like to be a little boy in the house he grew up in. When he died, we were just getting to the edge of being able to have some more heart-to-heart conversations about the things that informed the humans we became. When I imagine a world where cancer stayed away, Gramps and I would be having all sorts of deep, meaningful conversations. It's likely true that it is only because he is not here that I am able to imagine that.

My dad was the fifth born child of six. Raised by two Roman Catholics influenced by alcoholism, I know the expectations were high and the punishments heavy. The weight of toxic masculinity and white supremacy has led many men to believe it is their job to control the women and children in their homes, while also being the sole financial provider. I have not had to carry the weight of those burdens myself; I imagine them to be heavy. Even though I wish my father had raised me with a little less yelling and a lot less alcohol, I am grateful that he did not use his hands as weapons more than one time.

In my imagining, I see that he raised his hands once and was crushed by walking over a line he swore to his young self he would not. With that, he committed to doing better for me and my siblings. Change can be hard under the enormous pressure of a world that has trained you to believe there is one right way to do things. I am grateful for this moment that led my father to change direction in his parenting. I dare say it may be what led me to show up as the mom I have been to the two of you. I learned that one can question what was done to them and choose to walk a different path in the name of better parenting.

I also want to say that part of my deepest heartbreak for the two of you is that you lost this man when you were so very young. Not only because death visited you when you were just three and five, but because you two were his second chance. In his later years, Gramps dug even deeper into confronting some of the demons that had chased him his whole life. The two of you were his way to show up as he wished he could have for his own children. All he ever wanted to do was be there when you needed him and play with you. He left all the other details on the sidelines—to say he was smitten with the two of you would be a huge understatement.

On his deathbed, he grabbed my hands, pulled himself partway up, stared me in the eyes, and pleaded, "I love those boys of yours, you know that right?" Of course, I knew it. I saw it every time your eyes met his. I saw it when you trailed behind him, wood in hand, preparing a fire. I saw it in the fatigue under his eyes as he drove over two hours each way to make your birthday parties. I saw it in the hand you each slipped in his, pulling away to reveal a twoonie. And I see it today, in each story we recall and the love you've known without him even being present.

Yours in better parenting,
Mama

TEENS AND YOUNG ADULTS

Hello once more, Dear Reader,

We have reached the stage that a whole portion of society says is the worst. Take a deep breath and trust me when I tell you it is an absolute delight to have teens living in the house with you. This stage, like all the others before, was riddled with intense grief and outstanding joy.

The thing about the risks that our young ones are taking at this stage is that the consequences feel so much bigger. Tackling, driving, sex, substance use, all while trying to form a sense of identity outside of your parents is a huge job. Since we have been present for their entire lives, we are the safest place to argue with. We are the ones they will push boundaries with. And we are the ones who will be holding our breaths in the middle of the night awaiting their safe return.

When my firstborn son was just an infant, a wise woman told me that our teens need us as much as our toddlers do but in a totally different way. This was true for me. There was so much time spent being available and not needed, listening but not talking, and walking the fine line between sharing and giving advice.

Once again, I leaned into unconditional love, patience, and connection in order to be what my two young sons needed me to be.

SYSTEMIC FLAWS

Hello My Loves,

I am writing to you two days away from the 2020 presidential election here in the United States. I remember the lead-up to the 2016 elections; there were a lot of callous remarks from Dad and I about moving back to Canada should Donald Trump become president. We were all pretty confident that that would not happen, hence why we made such glib remarks.

You likely remember he was up against Hillary Clinton, and the outgoing president was Barack Obama, who had held office for eight years. The last four of those years were hard because he was up against a Republican majority that simply would not let him pass or bolster any of the things he wanted to. So, even though there had been a Democrat in office, there had not been the sweeping gains in the areas of universal healthcare, racial justice, or Supreme Court nominations that we'd hoped for.

With Donald Trump caught on tape saying his fame gave him permission to grab women by their pussies and an absolute lack of political experience, polls not in his favor, a good number of us settled back, preparing for the first female president.

On the actual night of the election, my firstborn son, you were with your girlfriend in Oregon; second born, you and I were out eating sushi, and Dad was on his way back from a weekend at the race track with his race car. Second born, as you and I entered the sushi restaurant, the radio announcer proclaimed early election results that showed Hilary was in the lead. By the time we came out, shocked newscasters had announced that Donald Trump was taking the lead and things were taking a grim turn.

Firstborn son, you were the only one not in total shock. You have a way of seeing the world that often cuts through the bullshit the rest of us believe in. You had suspected things weren't as secure as the rest of us believed. I remember Dad pulling up in front of our place on Buchanan Street and me yelling at him, "You said there was no way this would happen," before falling into his arms, sobbing. It was impossible to believe this is what America wanted. I now realize it was only impossible because of the color of my skin and the protections from reality it had given me.

Second born son, you came to me and said, "Does this mean we have to move back to Canada now?" A tear slipped from my eyes as I saw your confusion and concern. I looked at you and explained, "Sweetheart, we will be fine. And the people who won't be fine need our help."

I was in the camp of humans who had been lulled into a place of apathy for most of my life. Because racism did not impact my daily living, I believed it was a thing of the past. I was about to learn a lot about my ignorance in the coming years.

I needed to give you something though, my son. So, I decided to bake cookies for the neighbors and hand-deliver them the next day. This was for no other reason than to let them know that when the world gets hard, we still belong to each other. I don't know who voted which way. Most of our neighbors were less than chatty when we knocked on their doors, but it was about showing up. This is what I could do right away.

Then I got to work learning what I needed to know about the history of this country and how this outcome was somewhat predictable. I looked for ways to help both in our neighborhood and those in surrounding areas who were faced with real consequences of a government that openly admitted they saw them as both less than and expendable.

You were old enough, as the whole circle played out, to remember most of the heartbreak, disappointment, division, and downright inhumane treatment of humans during this person's time in charge. Year after year, lie after lie, driving us to no longer be surprised by his lack of humanity. There are reports now that things are looking impossible for him. However, we fell prey to that sort of polling information last time, so no one will breathe a sigh of relief until the results come in sometime after November 3rd. When the winner is announced, tensions will be high until the next president is sworn in.

I have not mentioned who the Democratic nominee is because, quite frankly, it doesn't matter; I am utterly unimpressed by him. The difference, however, is that people will not continue to be harmed by Joe Biden. There will be a chance for some healing to begin and for the structural change required to possibly happen. So, even though the country is choosing the "better option," it sure as hell does not mean the systems of structural racism will suddenly vanish once the Cheeto in Charge leaves the White House. There are many people concerned that, with the Democratic win, we will lose the majority of people who have been protesting. White people are lazily privileged, and these concerns are valid. There are many white women who have filled the streets with protests and believe their efforts would be successful if there is a "blue wave," as people are calling it. In fact, with this man running the country, a veil has been lifted, and we cannot unknow what we have seen. There is no racial justice in the United States of America. Once this election is over, there needs to be continued pressure on every politician and system for change to begin. Without that, there is really no way forward. My deepest prayer is not only that this country elects an actual politician but also that every voter who shows up at the polls continues to engage in the democratic process. For once, in the history of this country, I pray there can be steps toward honoring a shared history that is based on both truth and reconciliation.

Saying all of that, none of us have the right to vote in this country. It would have been easy to throw my hands in the air and declare that this was not my mess to deal with, not my problem. But the truth is, Canada has many of the same systemic flaws as the US. On the surface, it may seem like they are doing a better job of working toward systems of inclusion, reparations, and equality. Maybe Canada is, but the country is not free of racism or white supremacy. It simply just might be a more polite version of things, which in some ways may be worse. Many of my Black, Indigenous, People of Color friends have explained to me that, though it makes them sick to their stomachs to run into full-on racists, they would rather know where an individual stands than look someone in the eyes who is about to vote away their right to justice and equality. I also think it is important to note that I am repeating this through the lens of a white, cisgendered, heterosexual woman, which gives me a whole lot of privilege.

Prior to 2020, I would have sworn I would never become an American citizen, feeling as if it would be some sort of betrayal to my homeland. Now, though, I am considering that very thing. Even though I think the voting systems need a major overhaul and that you can make a change in many other ways, I also feel like I am a hypocrite if I sit here both complaining and benefiting without taking steps to participate in what is currently the only way to impact change at all levels of government. Today, as I write this letter to you, I know that I am going to likely become a citizen as soon as I can, so I have a chance to begin using my voice to further tear down systems of harm.

I also want to take a moment to apologize to you on behalf of my generation and the generations before me. This planet is sick. The systems are sick. Heck, right now, the entire world is sick from a global pandemic. We have known about all these things, but we never did enough to protect the planet for you or your children. As much as I would like to take my fingers and point them outward toward a litany of people and reasons, I, too, am responsible. I am responsible for not standing up soon enough to people and systems that happily went about harming the planet.

In 1990, I stood on a stage and gave a speech about the importance of caring for the environment. I went so far as to ask the audience how we had not done anything about these things, even though back in the seventies we had been warned of the damage that was to come. I was outraged then. Shortly after, however, I chose comfort over standing up for what I believed in time and time again. I chose convenience over preservation time and time and time again, and for that, I am deeply sorry. You and your children deserve so much better than that which is being handed to you by the selfish generations that have come before you. It should not be your responsibility to clean up our mess. We should have done that for you.

To oversimplify things, it is capitalism and all the ways it entices us into a self-centered way of existence. There is no regard for the elderly or the children who, in my experience, almost always hold the greatest knowledge and capacity for caring. Again, I apologize for this world that you find yourself in on the verge of what should be your most carefree years. I hope I can use what time I have left to put into place some changes that will make the world better for future versions of yourself and your children, should you ever make the leap of faith required to have some.

Apologizing profusely,
Mama

TENDING TO THE UNIMAGINABLE

Hello My Loves,

It was Saturday, March 14th, when I got one of those messages no mother ever wants to get. It was my soul sister on the other end, telling me her son, your dear friend, had ended his life the night before. There will be moments in your life when you think you are headed in one direction, then a freight train will come out of nowhere to flatten you and forever change the course of your life. This was one of those moments.

I had no words for my friend. There was nothing to fill the space that would do anything to heal what happened to her shattered heart. I barely made it up the stairs to Dad before falling to the floor, releasing the impossible words in the space between us.

This came on the tail of your aunt, just weeks before, trying to end her life unsuccessfully. So, here we stood, less than a month past, and you once again had to confront the reality that sometimes life gets so hard that it is impossible to carry on. I don't know why one person survives to get the help they need but the other does not.

I was the same age as you, my second born, the first time I learned that suicide was something that could happen to someone

I loved. My first love had ended his life, ironically on a Friday the 13th, just the same as your friend had. The serendipity of these two endings made me want to scream in total rage. What was the damn lesson that I did not learn that made it so you two had to live through losing someone who housed such a tender space in your heart? What had I missed?

To be truthful, I cried out in the same rage when your grandfather died. He was young, and you were supposed to get him until you were all grown up. That was the tradeoff I thought I earned by losing my grandparents at an age that felt so young to me. But here you were even younger, confronting death when you were just starting out.

The hard part of being your mother—the moments that break me the most—are the ones I cannot protect you from. I wanted you to understand death from a distance before it showed up to rob you of someone you adored. I wanted you to avoid knowing the truth that anyone at any time could be taken from you. I wanted your hearts to be protected from the earth-shattering reality for as long as possible. I wanted you to have a world that felt safer than it does once you are touched by tragedies.

I went down a dark hole of despair for a while, trying to pull some sense out of this. Lamenting about the whys, the what-ifs and the this simply is not fucking fair. But none of my lamenting changed the truth of what was on your journey. Your friend was dead, three out of four of your grandparents were dead, and you had not yet reached adulthood.

The art, though, of motherhood is being able to stand back to witness what you are experiencing, free and clear of my own drama and baggage. For me, it's been the absolute hardest part of being a mother. My stories are not yours, though, and when I clutter the space between us with what I think is happening with you, I lose the ability to see you in the moments—to know how these tragedies are falling upon you.

So, I have to continually pull my head into the moment and actually see you. I have to not get lost in the lamenting about my teenage years but instead, ask you candidly what the world looks and feels like for you. My own losses were not to protect or guarantee you any sort of pass, but they were to prepare me to show up for you with compassion. I can sit there and hold you as your heart shatters and rearranges itself because I know what it is like to confront the reality that life is fragile at every age and stage. I can remember myself as a teenager and what it was I desperately needed from the adults around me. I can do my best to offer that to you. I can heal my wounds by sitting with you in yours.

None of this involves me telling you any how-to. It is instead an exchange from one human to another, holding loss and grief while finding the courage it takes to step forward in a world that feels so unfamiliar and ridiculously unfair. Even further than that, when I meet you in your grief and listen more than I speak, I have a chance to learn.

You see, I was certain through a great majority of my life that there was one way to grieve. If someone was not grieving in the way the world had taught me is required, they were not grieving at all. I now understand each human grieves based on what they have lost. That loss can have many similarities and even some common ground, but it will look as unique as the human walking through the experience.

Coming to understand the productive or emotional griever helped me to see you, my oldest, grieving just as hard as the rest of us. There is the shoulder-to-shoulder griever, who needs a project as a channel for the pain, and there is the heart-to-heart griever, who stands with tear-filled eyes trying to hold on to a world that can never again be the same.

I know these events will likely show up in your timeline as defining moments—moments when you grew and maybe even changed course. The heart of it all for me has become that I never, as your parent, need to set you up to experience adversity because the "real world" will take care of that. My only role is to remind you that you are loved and will forever have me on your side as your greatest advocate.

Yours in grief,
Mama

PANDEMIC:
THE REAL-LIFE VERSION

Hello My Loves,

While I am gathering all these love letters for you, we are living through a global pandemic. Quite honestly, even as I write the words, it is hard for me to believe that is what is happening around us.

On March 17, 2020, we received our first shelter-in-place order from Santa Clara County. Since January, we had been watching China deal with its own lockdown and hearing of restrictions being put in place around us, but we were still basically moving normally through the world. Okay, we had started to wash our hands more rigorously and frequently, and I had started to see germs on more surfaces than I usually did. Mostly, though, we were still in the camp of thinking people were overreacting to this "flu-like" virus. Then I was standing in Trader Joe's and looking at the empty pasta shelves when I learned just how "panic buying" begins.

I remained calm and only bought one odd item, mango chutney, before heading to Safeway, where things had taken a turn. The shelves that usually had toilet paper and paper towels were almost empty. I texted Dad pictures, and he texted back, "Stock up." I didn't know what that meant.

I was still trying to remain calm, trusting that the shelves would be restocked. I noticed overfilled carts all around me: water, pasta, sanitizing objects, and paper products were the most popular stock-up items. This was the last trip out where I would retain any sense of control when it came to logical purchases. Fear was worming its way into my experience.

I am sure you remember or have your own memories of what that time was like. The first things to be canceled for us were trips to the hockey rink. We held on to airline tickets and travel plans for a few more days before realizing that people were actually dying; this thing was spreading out of control. It was not predictable or logical in whom it attacked, and the safest move for us was to control our exposure to others.

You, my firstborn, were set to visit your love, a ten-hour drive away. I watched you tackle the challenge with what I can only call grace. You wanted nothing more than to see her, but it was just as important for you to keep yourself and your family safe. So, FaceTime and video games became your next best things as you navigated what it meant to go past the comfortable point of missing someone and still invest in the relationship. I can only imagine that it was a terribly challenging thing. The world around us was talking about the young people and how they weren't taking things seriously by still meeting up with friends and attending unapproved gatherings. Parents were lamenting about the inability to keep their children from putting themselves in the virus's path. No one was talking about the challenge of having to stay away from your person, your people, the ones you were fiercely in love with. I didn't have to choose between my family and the person I was in love with. I had Dad by my side the entire time.

It's the place once again where our world undervalues the needs of children and youth and expects them to perform at a better, more advanced skill level than we ourselves are doing or are most likely even capable of. Older adults all over the place were performing the sort of mental gymnastics required to justify the risks they were taking while pointing fingers at the young people doing what young people do, exploring the world around them through trial and error. Hell yes, it was far more terrifying because there was a dangerous virus spreading. It was a familiar pattern to me of those with more power (cloaked as age and experience) telling those with less that they knew better while not following through themselves.

This was particularly obvious to me at this time because not one single human being who was alive had ever lived through this before, so how could any of us know what was better for the other? Science was coming at us with its trials and errors on a daily basis.

We had the phase where it was believed the virus could live on surfaces for 24-72 hours, so we built a sanitizing station in the garage with blue tape going down the middle of the freezer. One side was for contaminated products, and the other was for clean items. We put a brown spray bottle next to the roll of paper towels, waiting to spray, wipe, and transfer, leaving the aroma of bleach hanging in the air. Plastic held the virus for longer, but paper and cardboard contained it for only twenty-four hours. This started the leave-the-mail-in-the-mailbox-overnight phenomenon, and the de-livered boxes were left waiting out in the garage. I even went as far as to do the mental calculations of when the products inside would have been last touched by the virus-carrying humans who packed them. I'm exhausted just remembering it all.

I don't actually recall what happened first, the reporting of the virus's inability to really infect someone from the box on their front porch, or my own exhaustion at seeing everything as a potential hazard. Without fanfare, I stopped disinfecting the things that came to the front door.

Going out into the world to retrieve my own groceries for the first time was a terrifying event. It wasn't yet mandated that the entire county wear masks, so there were some humans being safe and others letting their virus spreaders run free. I was gloved up with my mask on, trying to smile with my eyes alone at every underpaid employee being asked to do far more than they had ever been hired to do.

In the short time since I'd last left the house, plastic shields had been erected around store clerks, arrows directing foot traffic through grocery aisles were put in place, and people danced a weird space of six feet apart in spaces without six feet. I wept in my car after my first trip. The sheer weight of having to be afraid of everyone and everything was something I had fought my way out of for decades. I didn't know how to avoid the fear when my entire family's health was on the line.

We made the decision that I would be the one to go to the stores. Grocery delivery was getting sparse, unpredictable, expensive, and morally questionable. Those with disposable income could afford to stay home, but those working below the poverty level had to risk their health. It also appeared our area was beginning to get a handle on things, which is hilarious as I type this because cases are rolling in at a faster rate now than they were then. People are walking about as if we have this thing fixed. The human capacity for mental gymnastics that support their own thinking and needs still stuns me.

Anyway, there I was weeping in the car, feeling covered in a potentially life-ending virus and wondering how it had all gotten out of control so quickly. Back then, I tracked what I touched with bare hands that would need to be sanitized. How I took my gloves off, when I took them off, and stripped naked in the garage before heading to the showers to clean myself. It wasn't lost on me that I used to complain about grocery shopping before it looked like this. I swore up and down that once things went back to normal, I would never again complain about grocery shopping. I laugh now, knowing this pandemic has impacted my whole worldview; I know there is no "normal" to return to. We won't ever hold the same freedoms we did before March 2020.

The days and weeks put more time between you and the one you love, my oldest. You, my youngest, at first chuckled at how little your life had changed with the restrictions to stay home, yet the weeks grew weary on you. Missing the freedom to choose when and how you went out into the world. As your mom, watching both of you, I was impressed by your resilience. It made me think that our out-of-the-box-thinking lifestyle had been leading up to this moment, where you knew what it was like to live far from people you love, find solutions the average person never once thought to look at, and possess the willingness to do what was required for the well-being of the larger community.

You, my second born, were the most committed to wearing a mask from the moment it was suggested as a way to slow the spread of this virus. Pulling the elastic straps around your ears every time we left the house, you were committed to making sure any germs that may have found their way into your body were not aspirated on to others. This is something I have witnessed in you long before now. You have had a deep understanding of what is required for community wellness even before you had the words, or research, to back it all up.

I think you were only nine years old when you came to me and said, "Mom, I know there can't be racism against white people, but I don't know how to explain it to my friend. Can you help me?" You were irritated that this needed explaining in the first place because of how deeply your heart knew its truth.

The time finally came when COVID cases seemed to be slowing and the need to protect mental health took priority, so we delivered you, my firstborn, into the arms of the young human who holds your heart. It was the longest the two of you had been apart in the length of your relationship. Seeing you drive off with her gave rise to a flood of confusing emotions I've come to know as a mother, where sheer joy races in right alongside debilitating grief. I saw your happiness light those baby blue eyes of yours, and I was no longer going to have my own blue eyes watching over you to keep you safe. In this new place of fear blanketing the world around us, I was feeling the weight of that in anew way.

My second born, I thank you for your patience during this time. You were there, trapped with your parents once again, in the house as cases started to rise. There was no buffer for our overzealous involvement in your life since your brother wasn't physically present to shoulder the load. You were generous in handling my overenthusiastic project ideas and the heart-wrenching tears that poured out unpredictably after what was a long, hilarious joke. You were phenomenal at telling me where your lines were and when I had crossed them. The confidence to speak to both Dad and me about the places we could do better is something I admire to this day. You know yourself well enough to say, "That is not working for me." And I got the chance all over again to practice not taking it personally. As a parent, I think it is easy to get wrapped up in being right, or knowing more, and miss out on the chance to hear what is being said. So, I thank you, sweet son, for teaching me over and over again how to hear what is being asked of me instead of feeling harmed.

As I write this, we aren't out of the pandemic yet, but I am already taking stock of what the two of you have taught me about resiliency, patience, boundaries, and stretching to grow. Sometimes parenting is less about having all the answers and more about knowing how to love each other well. This pandemic gave us all kinds of chances to love each other well.

Yours in deep admiration,
Mama

RESILIENCY AND MOVING BOXES

Hello My Loves,

Sigh. I am sitting at my computer surrounded by boxes as we get ready to leave California and move to Oregon. You are no strangers to moving. For you, my firstborn, this is your seventh move, and for you, my second born, it's your sixth. There was a time in my life when I felt guilty about all the moving around—that it somehow did not give you any sense of security in the world. Both Dad and I had pretty much grown up in the houses you visited your grandparents in. I also think there is this idea in the world about homeownership and stability being some sort of marker of adulthood or success. I don't think those things are true anymore.

You, my firstborn, seem to be quite attached to moving. I remember the first time you said, "I think it's time to move to a new house." I almost dove across the floor to tackle the idea clear out of you. You've also had some level of clairvoyance to you, so I was terrified that you were speaking a truth into the world that I was not yet ready for. And sure enough, a couple of months later, we were packed up and headed to a new house. I am not sure if it is a personality trait or if it is a product of all the moving, but somehow you seem to enjoy a change of scenery every two to four years.

When we bought the house in Parksville, I was certain I could get rid of all the moving boxes taking up half of the garage because we would never move again. Even though the two-bedroom home was only 1,000-square feet, I convinced myself of a renovation that would make it big enough for all of us to enjoy for our forever years.

Three years later, there came the phone call that would change it all. Someone Dad worked with years earlier called to check in and see if Dad had any interest in working for Apple. I know you were both young then, but let me tell you, Dad was the biggest Apple nerd I knew. He drove to the US when the first iPhone was released to purchase one that he would have to jailbreak in order to make it work in Canada. Rules be damned, this fanboy was going to get his hands on the latest technology so he could be a part of the conversation.

So, when he walked through the back door—a stunned look across his face—and explained this phone call, my heart sank. Even if my mind had not yet caught up, I knew if Apple was offering a job, there was nothing that would get between Dad and that job. You've heard the story enough to know what happened next. It turns out, buying a house has no bearing on whether you move again. Lesson learned.

Touring houses when we first arrived in the Bay Area was quite something. We were picked up by a total stranger, stuffed into the back of his car, and pulled from house to house—his prying eyes watching our every move. You both know we aren't your average family. Those who first meet us, however, don't always know this. He was expecting far more out of the two of you in terms of conversation and obedience. I was dancing the fine line between being rude and protecting your boundaries. I barely remember the houses or what they looked like; most of them were bigger than what we had in Parksville, so it seemed reasonable we could pretty much live in any of them. Convincing the two of you to pack your portable gaming devices and non-crumb-making snacks to pile into the back of this stranger's car for a second day was far more challenging than the first day. Keeping you from telling him to shut up and leave you alone was also double the challenge on the second day.

When I was younger, I was terribly shy and could never quite figure out why adults expected me to interact with them in their chosen manner, no matter what. Probing questions that held no value at all for me, bad breath too close to my nose, and demeaning jokes only fortified my commitment to silence. My parents were not present to stand guard at the edge of my boundaries, so it was all just terrible honestly. It's likely how I became both fierce and nauseated each time I had to stand up to an adult who felt as though the years they had lived on the planet gave them access to you in a way they had yet to earn. In the world of adults, if you walked up to a stranger and demanded they laugh at a joke that poked fun at some part of them that was outside of their control, you would be deemed rude and expected to deliver, at the very least, an apology. Yet here this guy was making fun of your then five- and seven-year-old selves and expecting your laughter in return.

To say we were relieved when the tour was over would be an understatement. Dad and I had a handful of houses we figured would work for our family. Again, moving to a whole new country and choosing which location would work the best without knowing a single thing about the place seems like a ridiculous thing to do. So, we did what all reasonable parents would have done, we turned the decision over to the two of you. Thankfully for us, you both picked the same house, and it was on the list of houses Dad and I had in mind. That is how we found ourselves living on Golf Links Circle with the bonus discovery of a community pool after we had signed the lease.

You both also know the story of the next two houses and how we got to them after being evicted. That is one thing that does not happen to you when you buy your own home. It was quite disruptive to have someone else decide when it was time for us to leave. The thing I think that made it both harder and more possible was how well we were able to make a space our home. The way in which we were living side by side, honoring each of our experiences, is what made it possible for us to head out and find new homes.

You both have had input into where we were going when it was time to move, which I think made the transition easier until it didn't. You were both on board and excited to move to California—well, as on board as one can expect of a five- and seven-year-old. That is, until the day you realized what moving to California meant and demanded to stay in Canada in a permanent way.

I'll be honest with you. When I said yes to leaving Canada, I thought it would be for a short adventure and then we would return to our homeland with a long list of adventures to share with our family and friends. You see, up until this point, Dad had never been satisfied with a job for longer than two or three years, and I thought, "I can pull that off." I mean, who stands in the way of a man having all his dreams come true? So, we agreed and moved.

It was around the two-year mark that you, my oldest son, looked me in the eye and said, "I didn't know I was agreeing to stay here forever." I am the mom with the hustle, working to make your life what you need it to be, and committed to your joy. At that moment, I had to look you in the eyes and simply feel your pain. I, too, did not know I was agreeing to forever. I, too, longed for the simpler life of kilometers and Celsius and poutine. I tried to make it all okay with extended trips home to visit those people and places we were missing. Living with your heart in two countries would always be impossible, no matter how hard I hustled to try and make it okay.

There was more than one heated place of emotional expression over this American life that, in all honesty, was thrust upon you at an age that you really could not fully agree to. So, we mended our hearts the best we could with adventures and experiences to bolster our memory banks and pull us into the place where we were living. Your hearts, though, kept falling in love with faraway people. Since I was raised in a time before the technology explosion, so many of my friendships were based on both location and convenience. You were living in the age of technology and were far more discerning about whom you fully gave your hearts to. Again, no matter the hustle I put into building local community, it rarely touched on the authentic connections you made with the people who were meant to hold your hearts. So, you kept on feeling like you really belonged somewhere else.

Then the COVID-19 global pandemic shrank everyone's life. Dad no longer went into an office to work. Flying to see those far-away people and gather at conferences was no longer a possibility, and you, my firstborn asked innocently one day, "So, if Dad doesn't need to be in the office, why is it that we live here?" A hush literally fell over the entire house as each of us retreated into our own answers. It was true that the view outside our windows was not the one we all longed for; when the ability to travel and connect with friends is missing, all we wanted was to be able to step into a familiar landscape and breathe in the fresh air.

The irony lay in the fact that neither of you was asking to return to your home country any longer. Yes, you wanted the ocean, trees, and coastline, but you needed the convenience of being with those who now held the biggest real estate in your hearts; this could not be achieved with the opening and closing of borders. So, we looked for a way, a place—somewhere in the middle—and found a home that, once again, we were all willing to say a big "YES" to. We moved closer to a border, next to a sea, and near a family who will forever be an extension of who we are.

So, as I sit surrounded by boxes and to-do lists, facing the third biggest move of our lives together, the feeling that rises to the top is gratitude for the humans the two of you are. Each of these moves has built in you resiliency, adaptability, and a solid commitment to your own joy. You see, as a parent, it is possible to give your children voice and choice as you live together. Yes, it is always age-appropriate, and yes, it is necessary to help young people feel they have agency within their families. It is this agency that builds a sense of belonging with our family unit. Agency is what gives you the courage to launch out in the world knowing you will always have a soft place to land.

Yours under boxes and tape,
Mama

P.S. I had to drop an addition to this letter. As we pulled into the driveway of our house in Oregon you, my firstborn, exclaimed about being home and imagined with your brother a lifetime of moments pulling into this driveway.

SPENDING YOUR UNEARNED BANK ACCOUNT

Hello My Loves,

You are both white, cisgender, heterosexual males. This is highest on the ladder of unearned privilege and comes with burdens of its own. Well, I guess it is not true that it comes with burdens because there are a heck of a lot of white, cisgender, heterosexual males in the world who have done nothing but rise higher and higher on the tides of their unearned advantages. The burdens I speak of are the ones that come with knowing you are at the top of the ladder and will need to continually check in to make sure you are not taking up too much room but are using your unearned privileges to get others in the door. The world will listen to you in ways they won't listen to me, so I beg of you, find ways to use that advantage to make the world a more just and equal space.

I know you might be recoiling at such a big ask right now, especially since most of our lives together has been about me not requiring too much of you as you made your way forward to deeper understandings of your own place in the world. I always wanted to preserve the space that was you and not interfere or mold you into something that was about me. So, there was a lot of space for you to experiment in, which is why this request might feel **huge**. It is likely true that the two of you were already aware that this is what I might be expecting based on how you have seen me living in the world.

You, my firstborn son, have always had the greatest intuition when it comes to human beings. You have always been able to pick out those who were not a healthy fit for our family. I questioned this more than once, but you still stuck to your knowing. I suspect this skill is something that will support you in finding those in any work environment who will be allies and identifying those who will cause harm. I know you have the courage to call out the harm and walk with your pride intact. You are a beacon of courage, and I have witnessed you, more times than I can count, being far braver than you thought you were capable of being.

You, my second born, entered the world with a keen sense of justice, advocating for yourself as soon as you had the words to do so. You knew that rules without reason were meant to be challenged even if they came from those who held power over you. Three-year-old you contested your grandmother's "my house my rules," naming how to right an imbalance. Then at the age of eight, you came to me for support when you understood that you could not be racist against white people, but didn't have the historical context to back your knowing up. This keen sense of justice and your capacity to take love and make it bigger before returning it to the world will be what guides you in a world that does not function on such noble principles. I know you are still finding what you need to use your voice. I promise, it is all tucked inside of you and ready to be used. Sometimes it's more about doing it poorly a few times than it is about doing it perfectly every time.

I know neither one of you will ever intentionally use your privilege to cause harm to another. But the hard part, the necessary part, is bringing a deeper awareness to the place where you unintentionally cause harm. It is not enough to say, "I didn't mean to." You must listen and collect the harm with the courage to grow and do better. There is never anything wrong with admitting the damage you have caused and bringing forward a humble apology. The stronger human is the one who can walk away braver and more committed to the undoing.

You cannot live in a white supremacist society and not become indoctrinated. Sure, I have been doing my work, but I, too, was raised right into all of this. And as a result, I have handed some of it over to you. We will need to spend all our days committed to anti-racism work if we want better for the children who come after you.

I also want to speak to you of sexism. It is alive in you. That might be a hard pill to swallow, but simply by virtue of being a male in the world, you carry this. In looking back, I know there are choices I made that perpetuated stereotypes, born of my own internalized sexism. So again, you will need to commit each day of your life to dismantling that in order to be leaders for those who will come after you.

I have tucked this letter farther into the book so that you have some time to feel all warm and fuzzy before I cast this full-on truth bomb into your reading. I do hope it will leave you with some serious food for thought and a renewed sense of the world you want to build for the generations that come after you. It truly is necessary in order to be a good ancestor.

Yours in courage,
Mama

THE GREAT VACCINE DEBATE

Hello My Loves,

When you were younger, we made the decision not to vaccinate you on the schedule that was recommended by the medical professionals. I would like to tell you an honest tale of how that all came about.

I know I was influenced quite easily by people in my circle who were not vaccinating their children for a host of reasons. The biggest one at the time was that vaccinations could lead to autism. People I knew believed that changes they witnessed in their children were most definitely tied to the vaccine schedule. There was also a bunch of literature online that supported this theory. I am here to admit I did not do much in terms of investigating the legitimacy of the literature; I was guilty of believing everything I read on the internet was true. You can find anything on the internet to support your opinion. So, I held the opinion that vaccines were dangerous without doing much research into the facts.

It was also true that, because of the efforts of the majority of the population, we were benefiting from herd immunity. This basically is to say, you were safe from many childhood illnesses because there were no outbreaks around us since the majority of parents were following the rules. At the time, it felt okay to me to follow this.

Dad and I had done most of our research around the measles, mumps, and rubella shot because Gump had become sterile in his teen years from getting mumps, and this was not something we wanted to happen to the two of you. From the research I had done, studies were showing this vaccine to not be as effective in the teen years if administered in infancy. It was at that point that we decided to delay those vaccines until you were closer to adolescence.

Fast forward to 2016, we were in the process of finalizing our green card applications. In order to stay in the country, we had to get all of our vaccines up to date. What did that look like? Eight shots each. The timing and choice were 100 percent taken out of our control. I would like to say it was an easy, peaceful process, but it was not. There was a force outside of us making us do something to the two of you that we had many years ago decided not to do. We had intended to revisit it but had not done so yet, so one might have been able to look at it as them forcing our hands to get back to our original plan. For me, in the moment, it felt like someone was doing something to us, instead of it being a decision we were free to make on our own. This led to more than one tense conversation between Dad and me.

Like so many decisions we made as a family, we came around to doing the next one thing. We did not have to worry our way to the end of it all. We just needed to do what was next. That looked like a doctor's appointment, where we weren't sure what would be required of us, but we decided that we would all go and see. Once we arrived, though, you, my firstborn, made it clear that you would not be participating in anything that involved a needle. It was one of the more challenging moments we had faced together. For fourteen years, I had worked to give you full authority over your body, to understand and know what consent was. So, there you were, eye to eye with me, saying, "no" to whatever was going to happen on the other side of those doors. Dad was sitting in his own world, seeing his job on the line and insisting that you do whatever they said. To say we caused a bit of a commotion in the waiting room would be an understatement. It is really hard to stay true to who you are as a parent when you are certain each human that can hear you is passing the harshest of judgments all over you.

You and I, my firstborn, stepped out into the hallway for some privacy—a moment for me to hear you away from all the prying eyes. Our compromise was that you would walk through the doors and hear the doctor out, and if at any point he wanted something to happen that did not work for you, we would decline and take the time to come up with a strategy that worked for us. It would simply be an information-gathering session.

Dad was not fully on board with me, and the tension was high. I think it is worth noticing how each of us carried the outcome of the appointment. Dad needed this for his work. You, my firstborn son, needed time. I was trying, with everything I had, to keep all of us in integrity with ourselves and with one another—each one of us so far outside our comfort zones. While you, my second born waited patiently for the appointment to simply be over. I wish I had taken a picture of the four of us squished in an office the size of a small bathroom. We had chosen this doctor because he was charging half of what the other doctors charged to do the same paperwork, not for his stellar abilities. We were the only white, English-speaking people in the office that day.

Looking back on it all, I wish I had talked to someone who had been through the entire process before so that I could have relayed factual information for all of us. But you will discover in life, my sons, that there just are some situations that you can't fully plan for. This was one of them. In the end, all that was required for this appointment was a quick scratch of each of our arms to test for Tuberculosis. Dad and I also got tetanus shots and referrals for blood work. The vaccines the two of you were to receive were not administered that day. Sighing in relief, you and I, my oldest son, made eye contact as the doctor approached you for the TB test. You nodded to let me know we could proceed. Our deal had been held.

We had more information and time to move forward with gathering data around vaccines.

Once we started to research together just what it was you would be vaccinated for, you were both more than okay with getting a few quick pokes to avoid having to deal with these illnesses that proved to be far more uncomfortable. At the same time, we all watched our scratched arms with great curiosity while we searched the internet to discover what a positive TB test looked like. You, my firstborn, were certain you had TB. You had some valid evidence on your side. You explained to me that every time you had made it to a doctor's office, you had exactly what it was you were there to be checked for. So of course, this time would be the same. I, having lived with anxiety for most of my life, knew that information and compassion were the best things I could give you as we lived the seventy-two hours between the scratch test and getting the results.

Those hours behind us, speeding down the 101 toward Redwood City to get our results read, I pulled out my phone to check just what the blood tests Dad and I had done were looking for. Typing the code into my phone, syphilis came up as the result, and that is the point where all the calm Dad had been holding in exploded. Dad filled our yellow FJ Cruiser with colorful words as the two of you sat wide-eyed in the back seat. "So, syphilis is your breaking point?" I asked, as we all exploded into laughter. It had been a long tense five years of trying to get a status in a foreign country that made coming and going easier. We were all cleared of TB, so we celebrated with takeout and more laughter about Dad's outrage at being tested for syphilis.

You both had completely different experiences getting those eight vaccine shots. For you, my firstborn, the aftermath was the hardest because your body's immune system went into overdrive. You felt as though you had been run over by a large vehicle. You, my second born, had a tender nurse who moved far too slowly for the anxiety that was building in you.

Fast forward to 2020 with a global pandemic and the world's race to create a vaccine that could slow the spread and protect the most vulnerable. I had moved from a cautious, delayed vaccinator to refreshing my browser to find appointments for us all. I did not once question the science or read the reviews. I simply jumped on board to do my part to regain some sense of normalcy in a world that, I dare say, will never again look like it once did. We were all able to get our shots at the same time. The second shot kicked all our butts, and we agreed over and over again that it was fully worth it to finally put down the fear of contracting something that could kill us or have us spreading it to someone else who may die.

I share with you this story of our vaccine journey so that you can see the value of keeping your mind wide open. I held an opinion, whether fully researched or not, that had me making decisions at one point in my life. Yet, as time and new information presented itself, I started to rethink what I had held onto so tightly. I was able to have compassion for myself and the place I stood in those original decisions while also being ready and able to shift my understanding. I hope, as you go through life, you are able to keep an open heart and mind to consider listening to those who don't hold the same opinions. I do believe our greatest learning can happen when we listen to those who hold a different opinion and remain open to adjusting how we see the world when we have more information.

Yours in vaccination,
Mama

LESSONS IN HARDSHIP

Hello My Loves,

Never in my wildest imaginings of the world did I think that we would live together through a global pandemic, let alone live through a global pandemic that kicked off with the death of your dear friend, Torin. And that this time would also include forest fires within ten miles of our home turning the air toxic and unbreathable, while we purchased a home a whole state away.

I am exhausted writing all those words down, let alone living through the entire thing day by day. No matter what life throws at you, all you can do is get up each day and deal with what is right in front of you. That is the advice I would pull out of all of this.

Before meeting the two of you, I had come to think that the best way to handle my own anxiety about uncertainty was to control and plan every second of my living. I thought if I was a step ahead of things, I was in control. It was quite unnerving in the beginning to realize I was not in control of anything. There you were, tiny humans, wildly unpredictable in your needs. I exhausted myself bending all kinds of backwards to fit you into the schedule I thought would bring the most calm for us all. I was still convinced I was a mind reader and could anticipate your every move, your every need.

We were planning a trip to Parksville back when we were only a family of three. It was days before we were set to leave, and I had already started to pack the car. I had lists, piles and things I could "live" without for the next few days, for the freedom of knowing it was tucked away for the trip. Dad was working hard, not even thinking of the day that was far in front of us. You, my firstborn, were eating, sleeping, pooping, and demanding exactly what you needed at the moment. I had spun myself into quite the mood when I snapped at Dad, "This is exhausting, why can't you help me?" He replied, "I will when it's time to go."

"But we need to pack ahead and think about this and take that and plan for that uncertainty and . . . and . . . and . . .."

He looked at me and said, "If it's going to take all of that, is it really worth going?" The trip itself was to be shorter than the days I had set aside to pack for it. He could see the lack of value in spending all the energy controlling the unpredictable. It was there that I started to lay down my needs to control and plan every breath we took.

You might be chuckling, all these years later, at your own memories of my pre-trip planning and organizing, wondering if indeed I had put any of it down at that moment or if it still was following me around. But trust me, it was much worse way back then.

The thing of it is, around any corner, there is a pandemic with unhealthy, smoke-filled air. There are also friends who will drive your car for ten hours filled with the items you no longer need to donate to someone they know. Sometimes it's as simple as seeing exactly what it is you are looking for.

Back in the driveway of our early days together, I was looking for stress. I was looking for a reason to worry. Dad invited me to look for adventure and trust. Truly, the more I focused on that, the less the other things mattered. Of course, every adventure is full of plot twists. That's what makes a good story, and as your Gump was known to say, "Whoever gets to the end with the best stories wins."

You will get to the end of this hard time with stories of how you lived months on end trapped in a house during your prime teenage years with your parents as your only companions. If you choose to have children, this will be your I-had-to-walk-uphill-in-the-snow-both-ways-to-get-to-school story that you can use to point out what you have lived through that they will never truly understand.

Yours climbing the snowy hill both ways,
Mama

YOUR FIRST JOB

Hello My Loves,

At the writing of this letter, you, my second born, have just started your first job. I cannot believe how quickly time has passed, nor how boldly you have taken on this opportunity.

It all started with me pointing out that a local coffee shop was looking for baristas. You and Dad had been trying to perfect the ultimate cup of coffee for some time now, so I thought the job might interest you. In all honesty, though, I did not think you would agree to all the uncomfortable things that are required to get a job. To my surprise, you said you were interested and asked me to help you get in touch with the coffee shop owner. You went to the interview with a mountain of butterflies raging through your stomach, trying to convince you that you would indeed perish if I did not immediately turn the car around and head back home. I know you will have your own memories of this moment, but I still share what I remember about it as a reflection from the outside of just how brave you are.

You asked, "How do people do this all the time?" as we rounded the first corner toward the Sea Perch RV Park for the interview. I tried to explain that the feelings don't ever really go away—you just have more experience surviving them so that it all feels a little less overwhelming. We walked in together, and I left you there with

Barbara, who would talk your ear off for almost an hour. What I was most impressed with was how you set a boundary when she asked you to come in the next day to see the coffee shop. You explained to her that you were only comfortable coming in once you were fully vaccinated against COVID-19 because of your asthma. I did not carry that sort of confidence when I was your age. She respected that and scheduled to have you come in the day after you finished your vaccination.

We spent a lot of time talking through the possible outcomes. Over and over, we covered the what-ifs and should-I scenarios. My job was simply to listen and reflect with you. I was to create space for you to empty out your heart and tread lightly, not with advice, but with evidence of my own experience in the world. I helped you write texts when you needed more information and gave you the trick that Dad and I had been using for years to get through hard decisions: "say yes until you get to a point where you can't." It has always helped us focus on the one next thing that needed to be done and not get so very lost in all the things that required attention. So, we focused on getting you your food handler's license as your one next thing. Then you would meet Barbara to tour the coffee shop, have a trial shift, and find yourself fully employed and heading into your first shift.

In writing all of this, it might be easy to think it was a seamless process by which you just stepped into getting a job. I want it to be recorded that this was one of the bravest things you have ever done in your life. Up until this point in your life, you had full authority over your time. You had not once spent hours doing something that you could not pivot directions on. So, for you to agree to go somewhere and stand for six hours, being told what to do the entire time, this was a **huge** leap from what was familiar and comfortable. I believe the reason you could do it was because you were finally ready. There is this idea in the wider world that children need to practice being in the adult world while they are still children so that they know how to get up and go to work when it is time for them to do so.

It has been my greatest mission to combat that idea by protecting your childhood and making it a place where you could explore, play, be curious, and determine what made you smile. I trusted that when the time came, that freedom—the time to build your sense of self—would propel you forward into the world. This is what I saw happening for you the week of your first job. You wanted to have a job, so you were willing to be all kinds of uncomfortable to make that happen. You felt ready to be employed and know what it felt like to make your own money. You were able to turn your sleep schedule around, deal with all the anxiety batting away at your brain (it was so bad that you puked the morning of your first two shifts), and walk out the door ready to learn from the people who were willing to teach you.

We spent hours after your shift talking about the day. It was most impressive for me to watch you finally see yourself through the eyes I had always watched you with—to know yourself as competent and capable of doing hard things. I heard you share your own increased confidence and name that you felt older already. I witnessed you have evidence that your anxiety was only one part of who you are and you could choose to work with it instead of letting it work against you. I don't think there are enough words in the world to explain to you the marvel it is to be your mother and watch you strike out in the world doing things you felt were impossible a year ago.

Yours in awe,
Mama

FOR THE LOVE OF THE GAME

Hello My Loves,

This one's for you, my firstborn. Your journey with hockey has been one of the greatest delights to watch. When you were born, your grandfather sent you a Montreal Canadiens hockey stick, which Gram then needed to counter with a teddy bear dressed in a Canucks jersey, sealing your hockey fate. You were about five years old when you actually started to show an interest in hockey. Sometimes I think it was tied to Gramps's dying and you taking his place on the couch next to Gram to watch the Canucks. Or maybe, more truly, having proximity to a hockey-loving Gram helped you to take your passion to the next level.

You were all in. We played hours upon hours of hockey in the driveway. I was the goalie, and you did all the things you could to score on me. Honestly, it didn't take long for you to actually consistently put the puck behind me. We had to get you all the gear to be able to emulate all aspects of the game. This meant many trips to the thrift store to gather equipment: roller blades to mimic skates, a jock, and even a suit for your away games. You watched the Canucks play while wearing your full hockey gear, so you could make every stop possible just as Lou did for the team.

We offered to sign you up to learn how to play, but you were not ready for that. You were happy with what you were up to. Dad took you to Sticks and Pucks a couple of times so you could get on the ice. We started going to watch the Parksville Generals play, and when they heard it was your first game, they gave you a jersey, a signed team book, and a tour of the locker room. You learned everything you possibly could about the game: its history, statistics, past players, current players, and so much more. I remember the moment Gram argued with you about a hockey fact. She was certain she was right, but you knew you were. She pulled up her laptop only to discover you had surpassed her knowledge and became the resident hockey expert.

When we traveled to Cupertino for Dad's job interview, we purchased tickets for your first NHL game. You and I pressed our faces up against the glass to try to see inside the San Jose Shark Tank. A man opened the door and asked us what we were up to. Frightened that we were in trouble, I stammered out a response about your passion for the game and you attending your first NHL event the following evening. To our surprise, the man opened the door and led us on the most amazing tour of the facility. We got to walk on the ice, sit on the Zamboni, visit the player's bench, and to top it all off, enter the dressing room where all the hockey gear was drying in preparation for the game. Nabokov was the Sharks' goalie at the time, and you got to put his helmet on. I don't think you spoke more than a couple of words the entire time because you were in total awe.

When you were nine years old, you decided that you were ready to hit the ice and begin your career as a hockey player. It was by far one of the most courageous things you had done in your life. We started with Saturday morning lessons where you hit the ice with about fifty other kids, taking the first of many lessons from your favorite skating coach. She was impressed by the speed with which you caught up to your peers, your focus, and your total determination. After the first session of hockey skating lessons, you were ready to join your first team.

You taught me so many lessons as you entered the world of organized sports. The first game, when I was certain you were feeling left out by not being picked to be on one of the teams, you were actually thrilled to be on an all-female team. You did not feel left out at all but instead felt included in ways that my schooled brain had forgotten to look out for. Then there was the time you came off the ice and asked me, in all seriousness, why the other kids were playing around and not listening. You said, "We are here to learn how to play hockey, and they won't even listen!" We had a long conversation about how not every child was there because they loved the game the way you did. Also, most of those children had been listening to people tell them what to do all day long. That can get tiring for a little person.

On your first team, a fight broke out during practice, and I thought your head would explode. You had studied the game so intensely and knew that teams were meant to bond and work together. There was no way that your mind could wrap around teammates throwing punches at one another. We decided to bring it up to the coach since you felt so strongly about it. He took you aside and walked you away from me to have a conversation that looked like one of those photos of an adult leaning over a child pointing a finger and tearing down a piece of their courage. You didn't speak up to him again, and I saw a piece of what you loved about the game fall away.

You signed up for all kinds of extra classes when you first started—things that required extra bravery. Many times, as we pushed through rush-hour traffic on the 280, you were certain you just could not play that day. You shared about having stomach aches and experiencing doubts as they swirled through your mind. This was when we came up with our famous family saying, "skates on the ice." I told you all you had to do was put your skates on the ice, and if at that time you decided you did not have what was needed to follow through with the class, we would head back home. Not once did you decide not to finish the class once you had those skates on the ice.

Your next season, you had a team without a coach for the first month or so. Another mom and I did everything we could to demand that the rink rectify the situation and give you all you deserved. The bureaucracy of organized sports wore on us both. When a baseball coach reluctantly agreed to be your coach for the season, things took a turn for the worse. He was all kinds of nice in front of the parents but tore you down on the bench when no one was there to listen. Then he stopped showing up altogether.

When it was time to register for another season of hockey, you declined and went back to loving the game as a spectator. We were able to secure awesome season tickets two years in a row and went to countless hockey games for the fun of watching the sport live. In 2018, a friend of mine posted that she had signed up for an adult hockey skate program. It was pretty much the same thing you had signed up for when you were nine, so I jumped at the chance to learn. In all honesty, I thought I was signing up to learn to skate. In fact, what I signed up for involved full hockey gear and learning the entire game. I was overwhelmed by the idea and wanted to quit before I even started.

You were thrilled to have me learning the game. Knowing your eyes were on me to see how I was going to take on this challenge might be the only reason I saw it all the way through. We both bought new skates and decided to hit the ice a few times before the class started. Before I knew it, we both had full hockey gear and were at the rink three to five times a week as you took on, once again, catching up with your peers to enter the world of organized sports. We live in a world that wants us to believe there is one straight line to success; you have taught me over and over again that there are many lines that take us to exactly where we need to be.

You woke up ridiculously early to learn with your favorite mentor. You volunteered hours of your time as a coach, again at the earliest of hours, and put yourself out there over and over again in the name of your own passion. You will remember the list of ridiculous things that happened that spun you in directions outside of your control. Each time, though, you picked yourself up, dusted off the lessons, and walked forward with a deeper understanding of yourself.

Hockey is missing where we stand now. The pandemic shut down the arenas and our move put us far from a rink, yet your phone is still full of podcasts and apps that keep you up to date on the most recent happenings in the NHL. Like that five-year-old boy who fell in love with knowing everything there was to know about the game, you continue to broaden your own understanding. You remind me, again and again, of the value of allowing a passion to take you in all possible directions. I am wildly curious to see how this passion of yours lands in the future iterations of who you are.

Always geared up and ready to play,
Mama

YOU WERE FIRED

Hello My Loves,

Oh, my goodness. On the very day I spilled out the story of you getting your first ever job, my second born, you also lost your first job. I wanted to bottle the joy you excluded on your first day off. We got blended lemonades and gluten-free subs and sat on a bench overlooking the ocean while you told me you were finally happy and professed your gratitude for all I had done for you in your life. It was pure magic.

Just two hours later, when you had finally relaxed into gaming, forgetting about your next shift, your boss asked if she could call you. I was on the couch listening in as she explained you were just too young and inexperienced to continue at the Village Bean. I watched your hands begin to shake as she filled the space with un-necessary words; a pit of despair settled in my stomach.

The thing of it is, as a parent, you set out somehow convinced that you can protect your children from the world. Worry shows up in all kinds of formats that make you feel like you are actually "doing" something to keep the bad things at bay. It's like somehow if you worry about it, you are chasing it all away. It has been my experience that there are more things in the world than a human can possibly prepare for. At first, you might feel a little bit helpless, but if you really sink into the reality that change is the only constant, letting go can happen.

I tried, and very often failed, to put down my worry and just show up for the two of you. It was true that you never once required me to "rescue" you; you only ever required me to show up and be ready to handle whatever it was that came our way.

I had never once thought there was a possibility that you could be fired. It was something I had never been through, yet here it was in front of us on the very day you had exclaimed you had finally found some moments of happiness. It's true that tears immediately leaked from my eyes, and I plotted more than one revenge plan. There was a primal piece of me that desperately needed this woman to feel the pain that she had caused you. But that was not at all what you needed from me. You needed me to simply hold space with you—to listen way more than I spoke and shine the light toward the things you had conquered and the lessons you had learned.

You were quick to realize that you could not change that you were young or inexperienced; those were truths that you had no control over. I think it was within twenty-four hours that you presented the words the owner could have used that would not have pointed any blame your way, showcasing you knew how to be compassionate and gentle with humans in the world. You laughed, then you carried on.

It is also true that you are now left with this place in you that is wondering what's next. It takes every ounce of courage you had available to put yourself out there and go for a job, and the idea of doing it again tires you. It is also cause for reflection as you explore what it was that you were wanting or searching for. Was it actually a job? Or did you have something else you wanted to prove to yourself? It's an ongoing conversation I am delighted to be a part of, and I cannot wait to see where the next big burst of courage takes you.

Yours in listening,

Mama

GROWING INTO AN ADULT

Hello My Loves,

As I write this letter, it is May 28, 2021. You, my firstborn son, are nineteen years of age, and I find myself chasing after the time thief who has taken the years and shortened them to an unrecognizable speed. I see you over there, stubble lining your cheeks and far taller than me, with a tenderness I recognize from the day our eyes met.

At the beginning of this book, I wrote about the challenge of moving into motherhood. I was in a bathtub sobbing as I realized this full-time job was not going to give me a day off, mourning the woman I had been before birthing you. Now I sit, watching the days stretch out before me with time—plenty of time—between requests, and I find myself sobbing similar tears. I don't want to be forced into retirement. This role as mother has been the best one in my life. Though I know I will always be your mama, there is a transition that is facing me.

You are an adult now. The goal all along has been to provide you with everything you need to launch out into the world as a happy, competent adult. Watching you do this is a joy that might actually explode my heart once again. The human you are is inspiring, and the possibilities before you are quite literally endless.

For me, now is the hard journey of letting go, all the way, of you and turning once again to try and figure out who I am. For nineteen years, I have had this place in me that wanted nothing more than to be available for you. I would adjust plans, say, "no," and alter my routes based on what you and your brother needed. Now what you need is for me to step away and fill my days with my own hopes and dreams, and I am absolutely lost as to how to do that.

Like that woman sitting in the bathtub counting down the days and realizing she no longer recognized herself, I don't know who I am in this next phase of our living together in the world, adult to adult. This is because my deepest desire is to rewind time and relive the whole thing. Instead, I will do what I have always done: take a deep breath and dig into the work that is required of me, so I can continue to show up in the world as the mom you need me to be.

I know she needs to be available but not suffocating. I know she has to dream of something that centers her. I know she will continue to drop everything to go on an adventure with you. I know she will stand in the same place of gratitude for the day you bestowed her with the title of "mother" and each of the lessons that came after that day.

Yours in adulthood,

Mama

"MOM" IS MY FAVORITE TITLE

Hello My Loves,

The two of you are more incredible than I dreamed possible on the day I met you. You challenge me to be a better version of myself and humble me into seeing where it is I fail at becoming that. Your existence has shown me that parenting is not about controlling a child; it is about unpacking who you are and tending to your own emotional wounds. You have expanded my capacity for love, not just for you but for myself and each human I encounter. You are not a better version of me. You are your own unique humans who've come here to this earth with a journey that I am so deeply curious and excited to see unfold before you. My wish, my one and only wish, is that you seek happiness always.

I would be remiss if I didn't share a piece of where my own shattered heart now stands. Through this entire journey of unpacking myself, I learned that being a mom—your mom—was the legacy I came here to live. Now that the biggest piece of that is over, I am almost paralyzed by the idea of moving into something else. I have convinced myself already that all else will pale in comparison to being your mom. Like the bathtub moment I shared at the beginning of the book, where I wept for the woman I had been prior to your entrance into the world, I am now weeping for the woman who is stepping into retirement from the career that took her beyond her wildest dreams. She is just as terrified as the woman who sat weeping for days. She is as confused as she was then about what is around the corner.

I am certain there will be unending amounts of joy witnessing the two of you stretch further out into the world of adulthood. I know there will be continued heartbreak as the two of you tackle all that life will unpredictably toss at you. If I have learned anything at all, it is that motherhood is a continuous journey of joy and grief, holding hands that march us all forward.

I hope these pages have given you a sense of who I have been and where it all came from. Mostly, though, I hope you feel loved beyond measure as you find parts of your own self hidden in each of these letters.

Yours in the deepest unconditional love,
Mama

THANK YOU

Once again, Dear Reader,

Thank you for reading these pages. They truly are what I needed on my bedside table when I set out in the world of parenting. My hope is that there was something in these pages that sparked your heart or buoyed your courage. Parenting is hard and ever changing, but you, dear reader, are doing an amazing job. You can find more tales of my learning alongside my boys at breakingdaylight.org.

In deep gratitude,
Shannon Loucks